GREVILLE JANNER

Janner on Communication

BUSINESS BOOKS

First published in 1988 by Hutchinson Business Books
An imprint of Century Hutchinson Ltd
62-65 Chandos Place, London WC2N 4NW

Century Hutchinson Australia (Pty) Ltd
20 Alfred Street, Milsons Point, Sydney 2061, Australia

Century Hutchinson New Zealand Ltd
PO Box 40-086, 32-34 View Road, Glenfield, Auckland 10,
New Zealand

Century Hutchinson South Africa (Pty) Limited
PO Box 337, Bergvlei 2012, South Africa

Photoset in Times 10/12 by Deltatype Ltd, Ellesmere Port
Printed and bound in Great Britain by
Courier International Ltd, Tiptree, Essex

British Library Cataloguing in Publication Data

Janner, Greville, *1928*–
    Janner on Communication.
    1. Communication
    I. Title
    001.51

ISBN 0 09 173586 6
ISBN 0 09 174168 8 (Pb)

About the Author

The Hon. Dr Greville Janner QC is Labour MP for Leicester West. A member of the Parliamentary Select Committee on Employment and on Procedure, he is Chairman of the All Party Safety Group.

Dr Janner is President of the Commonwealth Jewish Council and a former President of the Board of Deputies of British Jews. He is married with three children. He speaks eight languages and has made a massive array and variety of speeches and presentations in most parts of the world — from the United States to Australia and from the Far East and Eastern Europe to Egypt and Israel.

Dr Janner, who is a former President of the Cambridge Union, is the only MP who is also a member of the Magic Circle. He is Chairman of Effective Presentational Skills Ltd., a consultancy providing training for all aspects of presentation.

For LAURA and DAVID
Wishing them joy and health —
and with all my love

Contents

Part III   COMMUNICATION AT WORK

Part IV   AUDIENCES

Part V   PUBLIC COMMUNICATION AND THE MEDIA

Part VI   SOME FINAL THOUGHTS

Introduction

Communication between people means the sharing of ideas, the conveying of messages, the convincing, converting, controlling of others, individually or in groups, large or small.

Whether in business or in private life, good communication wins. Whether by word of mouth or by letter, in the press or on radio or television, the skilled and the schooled succeed.

The art and the science of communication is crucial to success. So why are its basic rules so rarely taught and so informally and so fallibly learned?

The answer lies in our traditional and immodest belief that we learn the use of words in our infancy and their application by use and by instinct. Result: second rate performance, born out of the trials and the errors of the amateur.

This book is designed to help create excellence, by collecting the professional tricks of the communicator's craft. It is for reading and for reference, for your enjoyment as well as for your profit.

Good communication demands the three essential E's: Energy, Enthusiasm and Excitement. Boredom is its enemy. So this book (unlike, unfortunately, most others on the subject) is for the reader's pleasure. 'Enjoyment' is the fourth E.

Colleagues and I enjoy teaching presentational skills to executives and to professionals; it has been fun to write this book; and I hope that the lessons it contains will provide happy reading. If so, then the book will itself be good communication.

The object, then: to help you to put across your ideas or your message, to any audience, of any size, from the individual to the gathering. To explain the techniques and the tricks, both directly and by illustration and anecdote. Straightforward tuition and checklists have their place, but so do the stories which water the desert of learning with the wit and the amusement of life.

The Bible tells us to 'forget not' the two essentials in life, 'To do good and to communicate'. In business life, too, communication is an essential of excellence.

Virginia Woolf said, 'The interest in life does not lie in what people do, nor even in their relations to each other, but largely in the power to communicate with a third party – antagonistic, enigmatic, yet perhaps *persuadable* – which one may call life in general.'

To persuade, that is the key challenge of communication.

This book is your guide to communication and to persuasion, in business and beyond. It explains how to get through to people . . . how to convince and to cajole . . . how to distil the essence of argument – to win without rancour or to lose with grace and with minimal cost. It examines the most crucial areas of commercial communication – with colleagues above and below . . . with unions and with staff associations . . . with boards . . . with government and with authority, local and national, and with Members of Parliament. . . . Then we look at communication, social and personal.

So here are the lessons to be learned, the skills to be studied. Practise them with care, and confidence will emerge. You will recognize the symptoms of nervousness and will discover how easily you can control yourself and your audience.

We present the magic of the close-up communication, together with ways of dealing with the mass media. Whether you communicate with colleagues, employees, with unions or with staff . . . in public or in private . . . by pen or in person . . . here's how to do it – with style and success.

The specific arts of communication through public speaking and on platforms, by letter and in writing and through radio, television and the press are covered in depth in my companion volumes, 'Janner's Complete Speechmaker', 'Janner's Complete Letter-writer', and 'Janner on Presentation'. So the main rules are condensed here and presented mainly in basic guides.

To all those who have helped me so greatly, my profound thanks. My particular appreciation to Leslie Benson; Laura Janner; and to my secretaries over so many years of communication, Pat Garner and Margaret Lancaster.

Part I

IN THE BEGINNING

1

Personality Wins

The ultimate weapon in personal communication is personality.

Scene: London's huge Albert Hall, packed with people from platform to dome. Centre stage, a simple podium. In marched a tiny, bald, 38-year-old man, in a blue suit with open-necked white shirt, beaming. Natan Scharansky, former Soviet prisoner. Behind him, portraits of other Jewish leaders, still in bondage. The place rose to greet him, for what he was and is and will always symbolize.

Scharansky moved to the podium and the audience hushed. For forty-five minutes this tiny man, speaking without notes and in breathless English, gripped us all.

Oratorically, he broke most rules. He stood still, but with his legs crossed. He paused from time to time, but without apparent logic.

He used no notes. His secrets: personality without egotism; message through story; and speaking directly to his audience.

For instance, he explained how the Soviet authorities combine lawlessness with outward compliance with their laws. When he was tried for alleged spying, they made sure that he saw the huge files of documents to be used against him. He demanded sight of a video film to be shown to the court. Eventually, he was permitted a private viewing.

The film showed a demonstration outside the Soviet Embassy in London. It was led by his determined wife, Avital. It included interviews with British leaders and with former refusniks. It was the first time that he had seen his wife for seven years and he was enraptured.

'So I told them that my English was very bad and I could not understand properly and they had to replay it,' he said. 'For the next four hours, my Soviet guards endured my video and I was in the company of my wife.

'Eventually, the Major in charge said to me, 'Enough. These

housewives and students will not decide your fate. We in Moscow will do that.'

'I would like to thank you – the housewives and students of London, for planting hope in my heart when I most needed it.'

The place erupted.

Then the story of Israel's Independence Day, in a Soviet cell. 'We weren't allowed to meet other prisoners of Zion, but one year in prison I had Mendelevitch in the next door cell. If we communicated with each other and were caught, we would be sent for fifteen days to the punishment cells.

'But on Remembrance Day, the day before Independence Day, we knew that people in Israel would be having five minutes silence to remember the Jews who died in the Holocaust and who died in the wars. So we tapped a message to each other on our walls, in Morse Code, and we joined in unity with the Jewish people.

'There was only one other way to communicate and it was very dangerous, but we used it. When Remembrance Day was over and Independence Day began, we flushed the toilets and stuffed them and spoke down the tubes and in Mendelevitch's good Hebrew and my bad Hebrew we joined together in singing down the tubes for each other the Hatikva, the Jewish National Anthem.

Now, that was communication. And if you have stories like that to tell, you too can afford to throw away the rules, just so long as you can be heard and understood. Anyway, when we teach presentational skills, we do not try to remove people's individual personality or style. They do that when they stand up to speak. The man or woman who is charming, bright and looks you in the eye when chatting across the table goes upright and develops immediately into a zombie . . . a lump of human cheese. The greatest key to success in public is to preserve and to enhance the personality which others enjoy in private.

2

Aim at your Target

Whatever your method of communication; – in speech or in writing, in person or by substitute, by telephone, telex, video – identify and target your audience.

Speakers treat students and trainees as if they were children, and children as if they were trainees. Academics bore conference delegates out of their minds with readings from their latest articles, scintillating perhaps for students, but hopeless for practical business people. Chairmen orate to boards as if they were mass meetings and fail with major gatherings, which they treat like boards. You must suit your speech to your audience.

It is always a disaster to talk down. Subordinates are as quick to resent as those who are or who consider themselves superiors. Trade union officials and members alike are equally sensitive.

I once heard that famous student forum, the Cambridge Union Society, rattle a then most senior politician, a Left Wing Queen's Counsel and MP called D N Pritt.

He held up his hands like a priest in agony, saying: 'Children, children!' The place fell apart and he was jeered out of the chamber.

Every government of every party knows that the people who will secure its triumph or downfall are its natural supporters. In politics, you can fall out with anyone else, but if you lose your own troops, you lose both battle and war.

In 1979, the Labour Party fell out with the unions and was driven out of power. Conservatives can afford to fall out with the unemployed, comparatively few of whom will vote for them. But if they clash with skilled workers, shop owners or industrial power brokers, they are in trouble.

Politicians must address their own electorate. Americans could not understand how Britain could be so ungrateful after the war as to ditch the mighty Winston Churchill, the architect of its wartime success. They did not understand that his grateful compatriots believed that the problems of peace required a different voice.

When Adlai Stephenson was battling against General Eisenhower for the US Presidency (or, as I heard him say, against the ghost of George Washington), he was universally praised in Europe for courageously condemning US U-2 reconnaissance flights over Europe. His comment, 'My trouble is that I am always running in the wrong continent!'

So before you speak, consider your audience and your approach to it. As you can never gauge audience reaction in advance – never, ever, as every stage artiste well knows – congeal your thoughts into a written speech. Work out your main points; put them onto cards; but let the words take care of themselves. Leave yourself flexibility to alter course, if your audience is not reacting as it should.

You must first attract your audience, or otherwise have it at your mercy, before you can communicate at all. In the House of Commons, some Members are affectionately known as 'Chamber emptiers'. When they rise to speak, the Chamber empties. Others attract through their oratory, their wit, their eloquence.

You must decide what audience you want and then strive to find it. Your quarry may be one person. A famous American newspaper woman was refused an interview by President John Quincy Adams; tracked him down to a river where he was skinny-dipping; sat on his clothes; and refused to move unless the President answered her questions, saying she would scream if he did not give way. In those decent days before Presidents were surrounded by security men, she not only got her interview, but President Adams became her close friend.

At least that journalist knew that her audience would not depart. If your listeners scream at you, then at least you have the consolation that they are still there.

Sir Ralph Richardson once pointed out that it is easier to perform music than words, because musical punctuation is absolutely strict and the bars and rests absolutely defined. 'Our punctuation cannot be quite strict,' he said, 'because we have to relate it to the audience. In other words, we are continually changing the score.' You react to your audience and to its moods or you will end up in soliloquy with yourself.

It takes a Churchill to recognize his own oratorical glory. 'Aren't you impressed to see 10,000 people gathered to hear you speak?' a friend enquired. 'No,' snorted Winston. 'Ten times as many would come to see me hang.' Audiences need magnets. Choose yours with care.

Then speak to your listeners. Watch them, hawklike. Start, continue and finish with eye contact, the precursor of mind and of message.

So target your audience; collect it together; follow its moods with your words; and massage your message into its minds. You cannot communicate without knowing what you are talking about. But it is equally important to know to whom you are talking. Listen to them if you want them to hear you.

3

Sources

Important communications need careful preparation. Knowledge breeds power and success. Ignorance is the father of failure.

Problem: if you need information which is not readily available, how do you get it, especially if those who have it wish to keep it for themselves? How can you induce holders to become providers?

When one of our daughters was tiny and we got cross with her, for some actual or alleged misdemeanour, she would push out her lower lip and darkly mutter, 'If you don't stop, I shan't tell you what I've got in my pocket!' With unerring instinct, she had hit on the inevitable human curiosity, created by secrecy itself. We actually wanted to know what she did have in her pocket.

How to find out?

Physical attack would have been ill-advised, especially if it produced nothing, other than delighted laughter, signalling victory to the victim.

So, if there was injustice, we tried to right the wrong. If discipline was required, it was administered regardless. And in due course, probably when the child was seated contentedly on our knee, we might cheat just a little and see whether the pocket was, as expected, empty of evidence.

When information is refused, try as a first tactic standing back; making out that you do not care; and then directly or indirectly beaming in, when later opportunity arises.

The converse is the direct attack on the apparent cover up. This approach is recommended where all else is likely to fail and where, in any event, the attack itself will communicate the problem to others and, with luck, trawl in both information and allies from other sources.

Kurt Waldheim was the Senior Staff Officer in charge of interrogations in German Army Group E, at a time when that Group committed atrocities against (among others) Yugoslav,

Greek and Italian civilians, partisans and prisoners; wiped out the entire Jewish community of Salonika, where the Group and Waldheim were both stationed; and sent British prisoners, after interrogation for 'Sonderbehandlung', which meant, elimination, murder.

The World Jewish Congress obtained minimal information and cast it into the waters of the world press. Reluctantly, gradually, but interminably, information was washed back. His autobiography said that he had not been in Greece at the material times. The clearest evidence emerged: he had been there.

Allies proliferated – among them in the UK, outstanding Parliamentarians from all sides of the House, including Robert Rhodes James, who had worked for four years in Waldheim's office at the United Nations and who announced himself 'betrayed' by the (now provably false) assurances that Waldheim had been 'cleared' of war crimes. Documents later surfaced, including a UN War Commission indictment for the mass murder of Yugoslavs, which resulted in Waldheim's inclusion in 'Category A', the top band of people for trial.

As with politics, so with business. Seek out the information you require, from whatever source and by whatever method you can. Do not communicate without knowledge. The arrogant mind is closed.

4

Time

To the traveller and to the communicator alike, time is the enemy. The luxury of lateness must be for others, not for you. As a start, check on the time when you are required to arrive, to begin or to stop.

My late father, then a veteran member of the House of Lords, was consulting his diary at a party. A friend enquired, 'Are you looking to see where you're going, Barney?'

'No,' he replied. 'I'm looking to see where I am!' For the busy person, time chases by so fast that you may (literally) not know where you are.

If you travel, this syndrome of total disorientation is inevitable. I sympathized with Prime Minister Margaret Thatcher, when – on a whirlwind, Far East tour – she said how happy she was to be in Indonesia. 'Indo-China, dear,' chided husband Denis.

Times change, datelines are crossed, jet lag warps mind and body. On top of that, impose the two ways of recording time – one by the 12-hour and the other by the 24-hour clock.

At the end of an official visit to Barbados (note the 'official' – it is designed to attract your sympathy!) we were driven to the airport to catch the British Airways flight due to take off at (we thought) 11.35 pm, which by our reckoning was 25 minutes before midnight. As seasoned travellers, we were to check in two hours early.

As we approached the airport, we saw the tail of a BA Jumbo cruising majestically past the tops of the low buildings. 'That's funny,' said our host. 'It's taking off. And there's only one BA flight a night.'

In our manic disorientation, we had misread 21.35 as 11.35 pm. Result: we were forced to put up with a day of sunshine and deep sea diving before inveigling ourselves onto the next evening's departure.

You may be sure, of course, that if you are early, your plane or train will be late. That also applies to meetings.

In one country in which events often start late, a radio comment-ator in its capital told me that one day he heard, 'This is Delhi Radio. The time is 8 o'clock. Here is the 7 o'clock news!'

Do not count on delay though, especially if you are the guest speaker. Arriving half an hour late for a meeting to be addressed by the Home Secretary and myself (among others), I heard the Chair say, 'We had wanted to garland Greville Janner. But he was not expecting us to have complied with the great British custom of starting on time.' He was right!

I was lucky at that meeting. The Chair kindly and courteously reslotted me into the programme, after the Home Secretary – a great advantage, because it is best to communicate after and not before someone with whom you disagree. If you have one thrust only, then choose the riposte, if you can.

So make sure that you correctly read the time for the communi-cation; insert it with care into your diary; reckon that if you are late, others will be on time, and vice versa; and if delay is likely for you, then prepare for it.

For years, I stubbornly refused to install a car telephone. I do not now know how I managed without one. Its main function, apart from keeping me in communication with the world, and the world with me, is that if I am delayed, I can phone with a warning, an apology, an indication of delay. That will not, of course, halt aircraft or train, but it will set at rest the minds of your host, your colleagues or your audience.

Once you do arrive, stick to the schedule. For instance:

• If you present or pitch for a contract, you may be given a set slot, probably sandwiched between those of two competitors. As in an exam, so in a communication with firm timing – once your time has expired, your chance is gone.

In law, delay destroys cases. If you do not exercise your rights within the appropriate 'period of limitation', you will normally lose them. In some cases, the court has power to extend time; in many, it has none. The sword of the law rusts, if left too long, in its sheath.

As with the law, so with communications – if you are given a time, stick to it. The chair, the meeting or the host may be able or willing to extend the limits. But they may not.

An Irish professor was asked, 'What is the Gaelic for mañana?' He replied, 'We have no word in the Irish langauge which conveys quite that sense of grave urgency!'

I once visited an African President in his Residence at 7.30 am. He eventually saw me at 10.30. When I was getting slightly perturbed, his aide said: 'Polye, polye . . . Slowly, slowly. . . .' In Africa, wise people do not rush.

You may also provide any of a multiplicity of alleged reasons why the time is not ripe for whatever communication or action you wish to avoid. (See also Chapter 24 on Non-communication and Chapter 26 on Refusals.) For instance:

'We really can't go public on this until after the next General Election/ Board Meeting/AGM . . . can we?'

'We really must wait until after. . . .'

I once tried unsuccessfully to induce Prime Minister Indira Gandhi to take certain action. She did not wish to upset me, so in the course of two years, she most courteously served up the following reasons for delay. The forthcoming conferences of Commonwealth Prime Ministers . . . of the non-aligned nations . . . of Afro-Asian leaders . . . and the (Delhi) Asian games. I got the message.

Finally, what should you do if you see that you are running out of time for your communication? Do not speed up your speech. Unlike a train or an aircraft, you cannot make up the minutes by increasing your pace. Summarize instead. Emphasize the main points but leave out elaboration or example.

If you are speaking at a conference and the amber or (worse) red light appears, do not be flustered. Either appeal to the Chair for an extension, or simply summarize. Do not gabble. Above all, do not omit your message.

Give yourself time to lead up to and to achieve your climax. Do not allow shortage of time to destroy the ultimate effect of your communication, which lies in its ending.

The best way to avoid messing up your presentations is to take your time. Thinking time for yourself and breathing time for your audience are equally important. Omit either and you reveal lack of confidence and skill and your haste will invite trouble.

At the start of your presentation, wait until you have the full, undivided and silent attention of your audience. Whether you are speaking to three, to thirty or to three hundred, the principle is precisely the same. For your audience to pay attention to you, you must demand that attention from the start, nor must you start until you have that attention or you cannot hope to hold it. Method:

- Unless the Chair demands silence for you, stand – or, if necessary, sit – erect. Look your audience in the eye. Command silence with body language. Hold up one or both hands if necessary. Rap sharply on the table with a coin, or tap the side of a glass. A crisp sound draws attention.
- Wait for silence and attention and under no circumstances start talking until you get it.

Once under way, do not be afraid to pause.

5

Boredom Gambits

If you must endure the horrors of boring communications – at meetings, conferences, seminars and other sadistic gatherings, then here are some rules on how to make the best of a bad job, and turn misery into laughter.

Like all the best delights in life, the banishing of boredom is an activity best pursued in good company. So find a seat beside a kindred spirit and the game begins. You need power, pen and a pad and you are ready to begin.

On your own or with your fellow conspirators, you make a series of lists. For each speaker, you record the following essentials:

- Time of starting. Estimated length of contribution. And actual finishing time.

If on your own, play solitaire. Award yourself points for your accuracy or estimate. With a companion, add spice by laying bets, modest or otherwise.

On cruise ships, passengers were invited to guess the distance which the ship would cover that day. The winner of the 'day's run' was the person who made the best guess. Why not hold a similar sweep on the talking time of your least favourite speaker?

Next: The cliché routine. Bored by an unimaginative speech, Labour leader, Ernest Bevin used to describe it as: 'Clitch after clitch after clitch!' Jot down the clichés. Watch out for the constant reappearance of 'the bottom line', or 'in this day and age' and 'at this moment in time', which you are helping to pass quickly. And then compare your list with your neighbour's, giving a point – or a pound, if you prefer – for each one that the other did not notice.

Then note 'good resolutions broken'. For instance:

- 'I will not repeat what has already been said.' This is usually followed by, 'I will not tell you about . . . and I shall not emphasize what has already been said, so eloquently. . . .'

- 'I shall say only a few words.' Or, 'In this short present-ation. . . .' Or, 'I will not detain you for long. . . .' This promise of spring is generally followed by a long drawn out winter of words.
- 'In conclusion. . . .' Or, 'Finally. . . .' Or 'My last word is. . . .' Or, 'Let me leave you with a last thought. . . .' Each of these harbingers of hope is generally followed by at least one other in the list. For those who are not playing the game, each false alarm will make the misery progressively more unbearable.

The next variation is reserved for those speeches which may contain something worth listening to and to which you are therefore prepared to pay attention. Look for contradictions. These are usually, but not necessarily signalled by such words as – 'but', 'however', 'nevertheless' or 'despite what I have just said'.

So, on the one hand the company, organization, or what-have-you must (clichés) pull in its belt, and cut its coat to suit its cloth; on the other hand, it must 'expand to succeed', 'spend money to make money' and 'give customers value, to hold or to attract them'.

Often, speakers do not trouble to present the contradictions, because they are unrecognized. They simply offer two alternative and entirely contradictory courses of action, each, we are assured, regarded as 'essential, vital, crucial' for the 'success of the enterprise', especially when considering 'the bottom line'.

One of my favourite companions at boring meetings is a most distinguished and witty author and biographer. As a matter of habit, he keeps notes. I watched him picking up the tarnished pearls, dropped before him at a recent international conference.

'Why the hell are you recording this rubbish?' I asked him.

'Because next year,' he said, 'I shall enjoy quoting to him what he said last year!'

So he has refined the boredom game even further. He entertains himself today by sharpening his axe for tomorrow.

'How discourteous to the speakers,' you say. 'Writing and noting as they talk.' Which reminds me of the speaker who returned home one evening and when his wife asked, 'How did it go?' he replied, 'Marvellous. The journalists were so enthralled with my speech, concentrating so intensely, that they forgot to take up their pens!'

Provided that from time to time you look up at the speaker and then back down at your notes, the speaker will be flattered. So eternal are the words that you have troubled to note them, if not for posterity, then at least for immediate use; if not for others, then at least for yourself.

They should only know that you are playing the boredom game.

6

Occasions

There is a best and a worst time for communicating your message or your news. The moment may be thrust upon you. Given the choice, though, select with discretion, then make the best of it.

As a youngster in Wales, I enjoyed the tale of the three friends from our town who went to the races. One was a coal miner, one a tailor and one a bookmaker's clerk.

Unfortunately, a horse went beserk, leaping over the rails and killing the miner. His friends were distraught. 'How do we bring the news to the family?' they asked each other.

'I can't do it,' said Tom Thread. 'I'm only a tailor and have no tact. You'll have to do it, Bill. You're a bookie with the gift of the gab.'

So Bill Bookie went sadly back to town. He knocked at the door of his dead friend's home. A woman answered. 'Is Widow Jones there?' he asked.

'No,' the woman replied. 'There's no widow Jones here. I'm Mrs. Jones . . .'

'Do you want to make a bet?' asked the bookie.

So it is always possible to make the worst of any moment. It is also easier to do better when the occasion is right.

An El Al airliner, arrived in New York. 'We have just landed at John F. Kennedy Airport, New York,' said the pilot. 'We hope that you have enjoyed the journey and that we shall soon have the pleasure of welcoming you again on board El Al.' He then forgot to switch off his microphone and continued breathlessly, 'Marvellous, now for a coffee and a woman!'

A pert young air hostess hurried up the gangway towards the cockpit, to warn the pilot to switch off. A smiling and motherly lady put out her hand and grasped her by the arm. 'Wait a minute,' she said 'Give him time to have his coffee!'

Not a bad motto for the communicator, that. Give them time to have their coffee. Let your audience settle in. You are a personality, not a telemessage. Whether or not you will achieve results will depend as much on chemistry and technique as it does on content.

There is, then, a time to laugh and a time to weep. So there is the right and the wrong moment for giving good news and bad. There is the right and the wrong time for asking a favour, for seeking a concession, making a proposal, winning a contract, and so on.

There is also the right method. The telephone is ideal for creating a quarrel but generally useless at healing wounds. The mass meeting may be inevitable, if there is no time for the intimate gathering. But the smaller the audience, the greater the personal contact and the more powerful the impact of any message.

7

Delay is Decision

When to communicate, that is often the question. In commerce as in industrial relations, speed is usually of the essence of the good case. But not before that case is properly prepared. In all communications, there is a time to speak. There is also a time for, and an art to, delay.

The American writer, Theodore Sorensen, said, 'In the White House, the future rapidly becomes the past; and delay is itself a decision.' As in the President's house, so in yours, commercial or personal. To delay should be a conscious decision, taken cautiously where time permits, but otherwise through experienced instinct.

If time is nature's way of preventing everything happening at once, delay is your method for ensuring that it does not. You and your audience must both be in the right mood. In so far as possible, the circumstances must be organized so as to produce the outcome you seek. While patience may be a minor form of despair, disguised as a virtue, the art of delay means making a virtue out of what should be a tactical or actual necessity.

Suppose, for a start, that you cannot physically attend a gathering. Question: does it go on without you, with someone else delivering your message? Tacitus once remarked, 'Greater things are believed of those who are absent'. So you could decide to carry on. But if, for whatever reason, you yourself should be the communicator, then delay is your tactic.

Before you decide to wait, however, remember another Tacitus epithet, from his *Dialogue on Oratory*, 'Eloquence wins its great and enduring fame quite as much from the benches of our opponents as from those of our friends.' If by any marvel you can draw your case out of the mouths of those who might oppose it, then do so. Sometimes, they may even be more prepared to give way or to go your way if you are not yourself present. But before you take any chance, make sure that if the tide is flowing against you, someone present will demand that no decision is taken until you yourself are heard. And if your allies object that the rules of the organization or custom or practice would prevent such delay, remind them that custom, when properly guided, will adapt itself to expediency.

Now suppose that the hour of communication is to be put off. How can this best be done?

First: remember that human beings are almost always prepared to be patient if they know the reason why. Passengers on an aircraft will willingly endure hours in nasty waiting rooms if they know that the alternative would be to travel in an unsafe aircraft. Left to sit and wondering why, they will soon bubble with anger. In place of their host's communications with them, they will convey their irritation, one to the other. Ill-will breeds on unexplained delay, especially if inflicted on busy people, working to tight schedules.

So you decide on delay; you explain it – and you hope that others accept it.

Ideally, the others (whomever they may be) should ask for it. You will then comply, like Milton's character who 'yielded with coy submission, modest pride, and sweet reluctant amorous delay'.

More often, though, you will have to make an active move. The classic tactic is to refer the matter to others, for investigation, consideration, deliberation and report. If a committee exists, you ask it to probe the problem. If none is available, you create one. Call it committee, sub-committee, commission or what you will. By invoking its talents, time becomes your ally.

As comedian Milton Berle pronounced, 'A committee is a group that keeps the minutes and loses hours.' Someone described a committee as 'a group of the unwilling, picked from the unfit, to do the unnecessary.' I prefer the Parliamentary definition of a committee as 'a cul-de-sac, into which ideas are lured, there to be quietly strangled to death'.

Committees, then, are both the creators and the precursors of pigeon-holes. Use them with care and they will father delay. But watch with a beady eye to ensure that the idea, the plan or the communication can be rescued from its committee, at your behest.

What, then, if the meeting or your colleagues or other audience refuse to communicate by committee? They insist on the meeting, the resolution, the motion or the discussion proceeding? Then you have basically three options. You may accept the inevitable and press forward to a decision, if necessary or appropriate by a vote;

you keep pressing for an adjournment; or you drag out the proceedings until an adjournment becomes inevitable.

Before deciding to call for a decision, you count heads. Company boards normally operate by 'consensus', which too often means that the Chair decides. A wise Chair tries hard to let colleagues believe that they have at least some influence over the decision. But in a modern democracy, the company board meeting may be the last resort of the dictator.

The Chair of a huge, growing and aggressive concern told me, 'If you want to succeed at my game, you have to take decisions. "You" means the Chair or Chief Executive. Of course you listen to your colleagues or there is no point in having any. But you decide and they know it.'

If you are one of the colleagues and you disagree with the Chair, then you may prod for delay. You will do so with care and tact. But you will bow to the inevitable, because the Chair's vote will be worth any number of yours.

In a more truly democratic procedure, though, votes count and must be counted. You tot up: how many are there who will vote on our side? If you are going to win, then to hell with delay. Vote on. But if you are likely to lose, you put off the hour of decision as best you can.

Delay by long and boring speeches and arguments is the classical tactic of the far left. Be brief, and the world stays with you; drone on, and with any luck, you and yours will be left to decide alone.

There is no need to leave this tactic to your opponents. But before you use it yourself, do recognize the fury that it may bring upon you. Worms turn, even those whose persecutors try to drown them in a sea of words.

Whether you and your allies will manage to avoid immediate decision will depend to some extent on the skill and cunning of the Chair, as helped or harnessed by the Standing Orders or other rules of the organization or meeting. If the Chair is on your side, or if you are in it, then the meeting may be cajoled into accepting the apparently inevitable, 'Look, let's all cool down and think about it. It's getting very late. A number of colleagues still want to put their points of view. Let's leave this over until next time, shall we?' Or (here we go again), 'Why don't we ask Geoff and Mary to go into the detail of this troublesome matter, and report back to us next time?' A new committee is born.

The Chair may also say, 'That's it, then. We have heard every point of view, at least once. I shall rule that we now come to a decision'

At that stage, if not earlier, you and your allies could call for an adjournment. 'I move that we adjourn this discussion until next month's meeting,' you say.

At best, others agree. At worst, there will be a debate on whether or not the matter should be adjourned, and that itself will help to produce the delay you need.

The first problem for the skilled communicator is to recognize when delay can be useful. 'It is very strange,' said Elizabeth Taylor, 'that the years teach us patience; that the shorter our time, the greater our capacity for waiting.' The younger we are, the more we like to climb our mountains and get to the top, echoing the immortal words of Sherpa Tensing, rejoicing at his conquest of Mount Everest, 'We've done the bugger!'

It is nice to 'do' whatever 'bugger' is troubling you. But if you sit back and wait, he may do himself. Alternatively: The climate may be better and the job more likely to be done your way.

When you recognize the need for delay, work out how best to achieve it. Then recognize that the achievement of delay is itself both decision and action.

8

Achieving Brevity

'I'm sorry that I had to write such a long letter,' said Britain's first Prime Minister, Robert Walpole, 'but I did not have time to write a short one.'

When Churchill was asked how long he took to prepare a speech, he used to answer, 'If it's a two-hour speech, ten minutes is enough. But if it's a ten-minute speech, I'll need two hours.'

Work at being brief and concise and your message will stand out clearly and simply. Few audiences have the patience to sort out your message from a cloud of fluff and filler.

The Ten Commandments can be written on a single page. The EEC Convention on the Importation of Caramel runs to almost 27,000 words. Both are rules and regulations, but their importance and influence has nothing to do with their relative lengths. If Moses had descended from Mt Sinai with such a document, he'd still be dragging stone tablets across the desert.

While it may be necessary in international trade to spell out all the details, avoid them in ordinary conversation. Use short speeches, brisk sentences, and brief Anglo-Saxon words – these are the root to understanding and persuasion.

Do you judge the effectiveness of other people's speeches by their length? People are always complaining that a speech or sermon was too long-winded. Try not to have this said about your presentations.

Begin by thinking about the overall length of your speech. Always reckon that it will take longer to deliver than you expect. Add at least 20% even to rehearsal time. Plan your speech so that you can end when necessary if you are taking too long.

Have pity on the readers of your letters and reports. At the very least, provide a summary of the facts and conclusions. Keep your ideas in separate paragraphs. Allow the eye to rest, and the mind will absorb.

When solicitors instruct counsel to advise, to draft a document, or to appear in court, they send briefs. A brief is a summary of the facts, with comments. A first-class brief condenses the facts, lists and draws attention to the main features of essential documents, indicates the solicitor's own views, and specifies what the barrister is asked to do. All this in only a few pages.

When instructing others, try to work on the basis of a brief. Brevity and clarity are partners in the business of instruction.

Next: sentences. Keep them short, comprehensible, and clear. If you go on too long, your listener or reader will forget the beginning before you reach the end.

The worst offender is the German language, where the verb comes at the end. So you do not know until you reach that final word whether (for instance) the person referred to has succeeded or failed, survived or expired! Still, at least the language holds your attention until the last moment.

A prospective speaker once asked for details of the audience, 'broken down by age and sex'. He received the reply, 'Yes, they are!' Break down your sentences, not your listeners or your readers.

Above all, watch your words. The shorter they are, the better. You do not need long, pompous, and ponderous language to impress.

Think of any great orator. 'Blood, toil, sweat, tears' – those are the words which hit.

English is a rich tongue. You do not measure those riches by the number of syllables in a word. There are usually alternatives. Choose (not 'select') the shorter.

During two presentational skills sessions, one with top executives, the other with professionals, I jotted down some of the long words used by delegates. You will find them at the end of this chapter – along with their brief brothers. Each time you are bored at (say) a conference, add to them yourself. Collecting other people's errors is not only a useful way to pass time, but you learn and practise in the process.

If you are suffering from a lifetime addiction to jargon then you cannot expect to change overnight. But you must start trying now.

A man of 74 was sentenced to five years' imprisonment. 'I'll never make it, my lord,' he wept. 'I'll never manage it.'

'Never mind . . . never mind,' said the Judge. 'Just do your best!'

So do your best through practice and get other people's help.

This process can be taken too far. I once commissioned a

distinguished academic to write a 'short history' of an organization. He did just that. It was very short indeed.

The book was launched at a ceremony, chaired by the President of that organization, who spoke for about three minutes.

Ivan Lawrence, QC MP expressed our thanks to the author, as follows: 'Mr President, I greatly enjoyed your speech. It gave me the time to read the book!'

Now for the words, in their particular order.

Attempt or Endeavour	= Try
Perceive	= See
Beware of	= No
In this moment of time . . .	
In this day and age . . .	
Currently . . .	
Presently . . .	= Now
Acquire or purchase	= Buy
Dispose of	= Sell
Bring to a conclusion . . .	
Conclude	= End
Demonstrate	= Show
However	= But
Consequently or therefore or accordingly	= So
Indicate	= Show
Envisage	= Expect, or see
Request	= Ask
In what manner	= How
Manner	= Way
Subsequent	= Then or afterwards
Proceed	= Go
Adjacent to	= Next to or near
Approximately	= About
Commence	= Start
Assist	= Help
It was necessary for us to	= We had to, we needed to
Obtain	= Get
Opportunity	= Chance
Assistance	= Help
You are able to	= You can
Arrested	= Stopped
This permitted us to	= We could

The remainder	= The rest
In order to	= So as to

The following are extracts from *Making It Plain* – A plea for Plain English in the Civil Service by the Central Office of Information, a helpful guide which I recommend.

Guilty or not guilty?
'Officialese' is writing that is full of verbiage. 'The futile drivelling of mere quill-driving', the Duke of Wellington called it. It clogs the thoughts of reluctant readers. It creates barriers to understanding. The Civil Service probably is no more guilty than businesses, local authorities and many other organizations. But read this example from the Civil Service Pay and Conditions of Service Code:

'Under Article 5 of the Civil Service Order in Council 1969, the Minister for the Civil Service is empowered to make regulations for controlling the conduct of Her Majesty's Home Civil Service. Instructions given in the exercise of this power are communicated to departments by the Civil Service Department as part of a consolidated Code. Such instructions stem mainly from two sources, legislation which binds the Crown or which, although not binding the Crown, Ministers have undertaken to apply as though it were so binding; and agreements reached in negotiation with the national Staff Side or with Staff Associations in accordance with custom and practice extending back over more than 50 years. Rules and guidance so issued are mandatory on employing departments. In some instances, the method of application of the rules is precisely defined, in others, the principles to be observed are defined and the method of application is left to departments.'

Not exactly easy to understand, is it?
Perhaps you've never written anything quite like that. But how often have you puzzled over what someone else has written?
Are you really certain that someone, somewhere, isn't looking at something *you* have written and wondering 'What exactly does it mean?'

Can I say exactly what I mean in plain English?
Of course you can. More to the point, will your reader understand exactly what you mean if you don't use plain English?
The reason for most of your writing is to transmit information or

ideas from *your* mind clearly, convincingly and politely to your *reader's* mind. Of course, you may have to use technical terms. But then it is even *more* important to use plain English to explain your ideas.

There's no need to sacrifice accuracy for clarity. Follow Einstein: 'I like to make things as simple as possible, but not simpler'.

But don't plain words mean more words?
Sometimes, but not often. The real aim is to make your writing quicker to read and easier to understand.

Generally you will find that plain English is shorter. One local authority put its instructions for drawing up contracts into plain English. The old instructions had 3,679 words. The new ones said the same in 1,850 words. What's more, loopholes which had been obscured by jargon in the old instructions were exposed – and closed.

And isn't plain English ugly?
No! The example of tortured officialese on page 1 is hardly beautiful! It's exhausting. You have to unravel the language to find the meaning.

One of the strengths of English is the way you can use it to express complex thoughts simply and attractively. Plain English is the way to show your mastery of the language and of your ideas.

How can I make it plainer?
Clarity doesn't come naturally to most people – it has to be learnt. Sir Ernest Gower's classic *The Complete Plain Words* is the bible of clear writing. Here are some important ideas he and others put forward. Bear in mind they are suggestions not rules.

- The first important thing is your state of mind. Your writing will be much easier to understand if you put yourself in your readers' shoes. The official who wrote 'In consequence of the non-payment of the above-noted account, an officer of the Board will attend your premises to disconnect your electricity supply facilities' had the *wrong* attitude. He wasn't treating his reader as a human being.
- Use shorter words. Write *try* for *attempt*, *about* for *concerning*, *more* for *additional*. Long words are often a sign of a stodgy style that sends readers to sleep.

- Use short sentences. Aim at an average of 15–20 words – even shorter if you can manage it. You can still be polite and, if need be, formal or forceful.
- Use sentences with active verbs. Write 'The department decided that employees should work from 9 to 5' instead of 'The decision of the department was that employees should work between 9 and 5'.
- Use verbs instead of nouns created from verbs. For example, write *use* instead of *the utilisation of*. Too many reports are full of these grand-sounding noun phrases.
- Sometimes it's a good idea to address your readers as *you* and refer to yourself or the department as *I* or *we*.
- Use jargon and abbreviations only when you're sure the reader knows what they mean. Otherwise explain them.
- Use a simple style. *You* may know just the right word. Be sure your *readers* will.
- Organize your writing to help your readers. For example, it sometimes helps to put your main point at the beginning. This saves your readers from skipping to the end to find out what you're telling them. Remember: readers are in a hurry to get to the point. They don't want to be stuck in a verbal traffic jam.

More help
Most departmental libraries have some books on plain English. Some useful ones are:

- *The Complete Plain Words*, E. Gowers
- *Usage and Abusage*, E. Partridge
- *Modern English Usage*, H. W. Fowler
- *The Plain English Story*, M. Cutts & C. Maher
- *Daily Mirror Style*, K. Waterhouse

Other advice on usage in my sister books
Janner's Complete Speechmaker, Second Edition
Janner's Complete Letterwriter
Janner on Presentation
(See page ii for details)

Part 2

TECHNIQUES AND SKILLS

9

Barriers

Communication means relationships – the breaking down of barriers. How can you achieve that essential? Start with the physical.

Interviewing a prospective employee? Seeking help, guidance or support from one or more individuals? Creating, maintaining or retaining personal friendships? Do not talk across a desk or a table. Draw up some comfortable chairs and leave the space between you clear of obstructions.

Addressing an audience from a platform? At least consider moving around the table to the front. Or put your notes onto the lectern but stand at its side. The removal of the object between you and your listeners has a symbolic and an atmospheric effect.

A microphone should increase the effectiveness of your communication. But do not let it root you behind your barrier. Unclip it from the stand, take it in your hand, and place yourself where you want. To control your audience, you must also control your apparatus.

Of course, you cannot always remove the obstructions. You may be restricted by a table, or you may have no way of moving to the front of your audience. The greater the physical obstruction, the more important it becomes to remove the emotional barriers. To relate to your audience, talk to them. Involve them and their interests in your speech, your presentation, your words.

Use the three letter word 'you' rather than the vertical pronoun, 'I'.

Above all, do not say, 'one'. That is the barrier word. In French, 'on' is accepted usage. In English it is old fashioned, standoffish and wrong. I and we should be speaking to you.

In short, remove the physical barriers between you and your audience. Avoid barrier words which suggest that you do not wish a personal involvement. Your communications can only benefit.

10

Participation

At the magnificent Harvard Law School, they spread the tutorial method out into the classroom. Students are expected to be involved in the discussion, the argument and (hence) the active thought.

My wife, Myra, who is a magistrate, recently attended adult education classes in modern history. She arrived home one day, enthused and delighted. I asked her, 'What is the secret of the teacher's success?'

Without hesitation, she replied, 'We are involved. She doesn't just lecture *at* us for two hours, but uses every trick to create participation. She asks us questions . . . divides us into groups, to decide what we would have done, had we been prime minister or king or emperor . . . how we would have handled the situation, had we been in charge.'

Add enthusiasm, excitement and energy and Myra's teacher created electricity, which radiated through the class and brought them – volunteers for the treatment, every one – back into the learning process, week after busy week. This is in stark contrast to a law school for the Bar, where teachers would read out sheaves of notes, which we were expected to write down, to memorize and then to spew back onto paper, in response to weekly tests and eventually to the Bar Final examination. Only one lecturer, a Mr Padley, managed to enliven this soul-destroying process. He did so by an unremitting series of personal attacks on the minds of individual victims. He tormented us with teasing and with taunts, with questions and with demands. No one took offence because he had no malice.

This method I have unashamedly copied, but I do not recommend it to any teacher who would worry about losing the occasional student, whether by intent or otherwise.

Not long ago, a delegate to a conference asked me a question which showed him to be of cunning mind. 'And when were you last in prison, Sir?' I demanded.

I was appalled at his reply, 'Three months ago!'

'If ever I ask a question with such devastating accuracy,' I said, 'I apologise in advance. It was entirely a matter of instinct and in no way the result of prior knowledge!'

So use humour, but without malice. Prod, poke and provoke. Tease the minds and shake them into action. Then you will get the attention and the interest of and the best results from your audience. Let them sleep at your own risk.

E M Forster proclaimed that 'spoon feeding in the long run teaches us nothing but the shape of the spoon.' Equally, force-feeding may suit the child in the classroom but it cannot overcome the adult's power to leave. The appetite must be tempted and trained.

So what is the difference between a good teacher and a great one? Maria Callas said that 'good teachers make the best of the pupils' means; great teachers foresee a pupil's ends'.

11

Think on your Feet!

If your mind works well when your body is seated, then why should it go numb when you rise to your feet? When facing an audience, does your stomach rise along with your body, your heart thump and your tongue cleave to the roof of your mouth? You need to study the rules on how to think on your feet and then force yourself to apply them, at the slightest provocation. So let us summarize some of the most important, as they apply to speechmaking.

Once you get used to talking upright, it is actually easier than doing so sitting down. Ask lawyers whether they prefer to address a court on their feet or a tribunal from their chairs and they will mostly choose to be upright. On your feet you dominate; on your rear, you are on everyone's level. So rise; forget that your knees are shaking; and stare your audience straight in the eye.

To avoid that eye being either glazed, hostile, mocking, or all three, choose it with care. 'Even in the most unfriendly audience,' a colleague MP told me, 'you can always find some old dear who'll smile at you! And if you can't, then plant one!'

If you look your audience in the eye, your own nervousness will at first go unseen and then disappear.

At the start of your presentation, then, take command – of yourself and of your audience. Adjust your tie and your dress before you stand, and your microphone when you reach it. Take your time before you begin. Wait for silence and full attention – then away you go. As soon as you hear your own voice, firm and friendly, you will start relaxing.

If you are making a form speech in which any false word may be slung back into your false teeth, you should avoid word-for-word preparation like an oratorical plague. Find all your words on paper and you will lose your audience. Instead use notes.

Notes should be brief, clearly legible and written or typed onto cards that you can comfortably hold in one hand. Start with your opening, so that your mind will be, literally, reminded of your first words, even if these are only 'Ladies and Gentlemen'. If you run into protocol, take a leaf out of the toastmaster's book and (if necessary with his help) list your listeners: 'Mr President, My Lord Mayor, My Lords, Ladies and Gentlemen. . . .'

Next, structure your speech. Work out its main points and put each one onto a separate card. Create the skeleton of your presentation and flesh it out with words, to fit both the audience and its reaction.

I once heard the late and redoubtable Lord (Manny) Shinwell, then aged 94, deliver a fantastic oratorical performance in Trafalgar Square. He used no notes. I later asked him whether he ever prepared his speeches.

'I work out half a dozen ideas,' he said, 'and then hope for the best. Usually, the words will cascade out when the time comes. Sometimes, they dry up. And that's the challenge of public speaking.' I never saw Shinwell lose on his feet. But those who read their speeches seldom win.

In Parliament, only front benchers at the despatch box are allowed to read their speeches. The rest of us may use notes. If a colleague breaks this rule, someone on the other side is almost certain to shout out, 'Reading!' – which may sound juvenile when you listen to Parliamentary Question Time on the radio but it does prevent MPs from being driven out of the Chamber by boredom.

In the US Congress, you may submit your speeches to be inserted into the record. In our legislature, prepared monotonies designed for repetition in the local press are not appreciated. You must speak to your audience and ignore the external echoes.

Once you have prepared and noted the body of your speech, sketch out its ending. Your first and your last words are the most important. The first create the atmosphere and the last leave your listeners with your message in their minds.

Most untrained communicators lower their voice at the end of most sentences and leave their audience on some such unoriginal and crashing anti-climax as, 'Thank you very much for listening to me.' The idea of reaching your climax before your intercourse begins is a curious reversal of nature! Your audience, sir or madam, should be thanking you for addressing them. So lift up your ending; pause; nod or bow; then stay still and await the applause which you know you have earned.

The key to confidence is to know both your subject and your

audience. The former you can study in advance; the latter will depend not only on persons but on mood. Ask professional performers and they will tell you: 'A story or a joke which brings the house down one night may die on the next.' That is the challenge of performing.

As a speechmaker, you perform from your own script. If you prepare your speech and use your notes as pointers, not crutches, then you are ready to think on your feet. No heckler can throw you off your course, if it is already variable; no interrupter can destroy your concentration if your mind is on your ideas rather than your words.

Speakers always have a vast advantage over those who would destroy them. The audience has come to hear them? Then the many will not appreciate disturbance from a few.

Words matter and gestures detract from their impact. So keep still and if you do not know what to do with your hands, press your fingers on the table or on to the lectern, or put your hands behind your back.

To hold your audience, vary your pace and your material. Watch your listeners and when their attention wanders, chase them – with an anecdote or an analogy, a joke or a story. Cast your beady eyes at the man who yawns. And avoid people talking while you are. Or just stare at them. If you are free to move – with or without a wandering microphone – stroll in their direction and they will soon stop talking. If your presentation deserves attention, make sure that you get it.

If you cannot be heard, then adjust your voice to the acoustics. Move nearer to the microhone – or hold it closer to your mouth. Or just imagine that the man at the back of the room is deaf. He may be.

I once studied at Harvard Law School under a brilliant and eccentric international lawyer, Judge Manley Hudson. When he could not hear a student, he would yell out, 'Take your voice and throw it against the wall and make it' – here he paused for both breath and effect and then bellowed out – 'B - O - U - N - C - E off!' Hyperbole, of course, but better your words should be loudly heard than not at all.

Once you know these rules, practise them on any willing victims you can find. You are invited to your local Rotary Club lunch? Then accept. You hear of a series of lectures at your local Women's Institute or Church Council? Then offer to give one on your speciality.

Or get yourself trained by experts. Armed, for instance, with see-yourself-hear-yourself video and recording machinery, you can learn more in a couple of compressed and comparatively painless days than you could from a lifetime of error, causing on each occasion suffering not only to yourself but to your hapless listeners, who are probably undeserving of such treatment.

Too many speakers are oratorical sado-masochists. Which explains why audiences retreat from lectures and meetings to the comparative safety of radio and the box. At least if a presenter is not switched on, they can forthwith switch him off.

So if you wish to be invited back, prepare and practise to think on your feet. As one fuel expert put it, 'If the speaker cannot strike oil, then we shall do our best to see that he stops boring!' Conversely, if you speak well on your feet, others will think well of your case. Speechmaking is an art and the fact that too few executives are prepared to devote enough time to its study gives *you* a vast advantage if you are prepared to be the exception to this sad rule.

12

Style, Appearance and Body Talk

The style of any communication by any medium is the key to success. For the individual, style, appearance and body movements talk as effectively as the tongue.

Style should be individual, even when it is corporate. Public relations outfits are paid fortunes to evolve distinctive styles of presentation. Logos, trade marks, the make-up of a product or of its box, bottle or other container . . . all combining to convey a message which potential clients or customers will notice, remember and applaud. Notepaper, the 'topping and tailing' of letters, neatness of typing, accuracy of spelling, grammatical decencies – all add up to acceptable and skilled styling.

Appearances count as much in self-presentation. Appropriate dress for the occasion includes immaculate cleanliness – how unmentionable are the odours of bodies, dirt under nails or bad breath. Appearances, in the widest sense, should attract not repel, conquer distance not induce the wish to create it.

On radio, as by telephone, all depends on voice. Warmth, sincerity, enthusiasm, conviction – you have no other way to show it. Detail of inflection is worth study and practice.

On television, visual details count. It is not enough to wear plain pastel colours which do not 'move'. You must watch your own movements because each is writ large. The hand in front of the mouth, the fingers scratching the back, the surreptitious tucking in of shirt or pulling up of socks. . . . And observe the specks of dandruff, the ridged hump of jacket not pulled down.

Your appearance talks, along with your body. Eye contact masks nervousness. On TV, if you get the right 'eye line', you will appear to be looking at your inverviewer or audience. Mistakes indicate the shifty, the cunning, the insincere.

So look your audience in the eye. Sit back in your chair, relaxed but upright. Stand with feet slightly apart, at ease, but without slouching.

Use gestures sparingly, to emphasise or to add and never to punctuate or beat time. Hold up fingers to count . . . reach out arms to signify breadth . . . but never pound the table or claw the air.

Get your appearance right and your body talk under control and you can then control your nerves. All people have and suffer from nerves. The performer in any sphere needs nervous tension to release adrenalin, to sharpen and tone up the functions of body and mind. So greet your anxiety as an ally. Accept that nerves are an inevitable necessity. Then control them.

Start with the confidence of full preparation. Then recognize that once you hear the sound of your voice, you will stop worrying whether your vocal chords will freeze. Remember: Your feelings are internal and your audience will not know of them unless you are inexperienced enough to tell them, either in words or with your body.

Stand or sit still and speak up. Establish and keep eye contact with your audience. Measure your words, and pause (see Chapters 15 and 16). Avoid the 'er' and 'um' and your style, your appearance and your body will talk as eloquently as your words.

You are then set to think on your feet.

13

Turning Problems to Success

There are times for apology, merited or otherwise (see also Chapter 18). Genuine, intentional hurt demands unqualified regrets. And you may respond to an unintentionally thoughtless or uninformed question by saying: 'I'm sorry, it's my fault. I didn't explain it clearly enough before. Let me try again . . .' But do not apologize unintentionally. In the words of that old song: emphasize the positive.

A terrified speaker may begin, 'I have never addressed an audience like this before. You must forgive me if I make mistakes.' Terrible.

Or, 'I'm only a technologist/accountant/scientist (or whatever). So if I bore you, please forgive me.' Certainly not. There is no reason why you should be boring, still less why you should threaten to be.

Now try positive openings:

- 'It is a challenge for me to be invited to speak for the first time to an audience of. . . . On the one hand, I look forward to presenting you with some new ideas in my field, and showing you how they relate to yours. And then both during question time and discussion and dinner afterwards, it will be my pleasure to listen to and to learn from you. We have much knowledge and experience to exchange – to our mutual benefit.'
- 'My expertise is in the area of. . . . Yours is in. . . . Today we have the chance to put the two together. If you drop into your jargon during question time or discussion or dinner afterwards, I shall not hesitate to tell you and to ask for explanations. Please return the compliment by signalling to me if I unwittingly use expressions, language or – still worse – initials, which are part of my everyday chat and vocabulary but which are not clear to you.'

No note of apology. None. You have nothing for which to

apologize. You are bringing them what they do not possess – a new area of knowledge. Otherwise, they would neither have asked you to speak nor attended your talk.

Do you play bridge? Then if your game is genuinely bad, it is wise to polish it up before you enter contests with good players or they may think that you are as stupid in your business or profession as you are at the bridge table.

In general, though, it is not bright to play with or against people whose own talents are unknown, 'Bridge is not my line. Forgive me if I make mistakes.' Theirs may be worse.

So study the techniques and put them into practice. Use a positive approach both to the learning and to the use of your skills as a communicator. Instead of playing down your ability or role, polish it up.

Now consider how you can turn a potential negative into a selling positive.

Suppose, first, that yours is a small undertaking, with limited resources. Your approach must be, 'We have deliberately kept our operation compact and highly specialized. We work with specialists/sub-contractors, carefully selected for our firm's/customers' requirements. One of our team personally takes charge of each account/order . . . so we provide top personalized, specialized, professional service at minimal cost to the client.'

The alternative, for the larger outfit is to emphasize precisely the opposite, 'We have within our own firm/company/resources a complete range of specialization that our clients need – immediately available. I will be responsible for co-ordinating your work/order . . . so you will have all the advantages of personal attention and of the highly specialized service of our organization.'

Now suppose that your charge is high, compared to those of competitors, large or small. Do not apologize. 'Of course we charge out our executives'/partners' time for our products at a sensible rate.'

If you are talking to your own team – superiors or subordinates, colleagues or sales people, or, for that matter, workforce or trade unions – optimism is a trademark of leadership. Even if you feel depressed, do not show it. If you must present bad news, then do so, frankly and with courage. But if the dark cloud with which you must envelop your talk contains even the ghost of brighter lining, then open it up. At least try to end with a tinge of hope.

Forced to announce redundancies? Then explain how you

propose to retain a viable workforce and to build the business. Reporting poor results? Then explain their reason and what you are doing to prevent recurrence.

God once announced to his priests of all religions that in two days a new flood would descend upon the world and engulf all people. At this horrendous news, the Pope sent an immediate message to his Cardinals. 'Pray,' he proclaimed. 'Let us all pray together that we may be redeemed.'

The Archbishop of Canterbury sent word to his Archbishops and Bishops, priests and curates. 'Toll the church bells and call your people together,' he commanded. 'Let us pray for forgiveness for our sins and that we may achieve everlasting life in the world to come.'

The Chief Rabbis of Israel faxed immediate word to the Jewish communities of the world. 'Brothers and sisters,' it read, 'you have 48 hours to learn to live under water!'

Which brings us back to the song with which we began. After accentuating the positive and eliminating the negative and leaving as little as possible in between, it continues: 'To illustrate, that last remark, take Jonah in the Whale, Noah in the Ark.'

Jonah arranged the most positive exit in human history. Noah rejected the concept of living under water but instead organized the most successful flotation on record.

14

Tripping over your Tongue

The tongue is the communicator's main danger. The runner who trips over his own feet must pick himself up and get back into the race. The speaker who falls over his words must be equally agile.

We all do it. My own Parliamentary moment of dismay came in December 1986. I asked for an emergency debate. The Marconi factory in my constituency had created and wished to manufacture a simulator, a brilliant machine for the training of pilots of Harrier aircraft. They could practise piloting without entering the cockpit. But the Ministry of Defence was proposing to buy a rival simulator, designed and manufactured in the USA.

I announced the need for a debate on the Marconi Harrier 'stimulator'. Stimulator? The place exploded with laughter. A Tory bellowed out, 'I want one for Christmas!'

I joked that I was at least glad that I had at last stimulated the Government into some sort of action. That brought a laugh, but not as good as the many ripostes which I thought of afterwards and wished I had made at the time. A pity that I did not send vibrations through the House! But I did have the presence of mind to apologize; to say that of course I was referring to the Marconi 'simulator', and to continue as unabashed as possible with my (alas, unsuccessful) effort to keep employment in my constituency and this area of technology in the UK.

If your error is comic, then, join in the laughter. Those who laugh at themselves will bring others with them. Which is much easier to do if you are among your peers.

When we teach presentational skills, we always try to combine people at the same level, however mighty, however modest. It is far easier to pick yourself up from the ground if those above you are not standing critically by. Equally, oratorical death by your own hand is bearable when you are among equals, but insufferable before the eyes of those below.

Not long ago, we were teaching presentational skills to a group of senior executives. To our dismay and theirs, the Chairman of the company – a distinguished but non-practising member of the House of Lords, emerged through the door. 'You don't mind my sitting in, do you?' he asked.

As he was the boss, I could scarcely refuse. 'Fine,' I said. 'But you won't mind joining in, will you? This is not a spectator sport. . . .'

He was an excellent sport and we plunged him before the cameras. By the end of the day, he became the exception to our rule of equality.

The next morning, he returned for more. I called on him to make a brief speech on a business related topic and asked a bright young executive to introduce him, which he did, thus, 'It is a very great pleasure to present to you, his extinguished lordship. . . .'

They say that a Member of Parliament is distinguished, but an *ex*-Member is *ex*tinguished.

Happily, the Chairman realized that the joke was on him. The error was forgiven, but has never been forgotten.

If you make a mistake in speech, you have a number of possible courses of action or of inaction:

- You can carry straight on. Like actors who fluff, ad lib . . . ignore the error and your audience will probably miss it.
- Pick yourself up and apologize. 'I'll say that again . . .' 'Sorry . . . what I meant was . . .'
- Laugh, shrug and try to pile a deliberate laugh onto one born in error.

Unfortunately, this sort of choice has to be taken instantaneously. Even when you have learned to pause to think, you have seconds only. Experience will teach you which way to plunge. Sometimes you will get it right. As for the rest, join the club. Think of the pleasure that your error will have given to others. Let it stimulate you to greater effort, so that you enjoy the vibrations of your unsimulated demise!

15

Breathing Time

The best way to avoid messing up your presentations is to take your time. Breathing time for yourself and thinking time for your audience are equally important. Omit either and you reveal lack of confidence and skill and your haste will invite trouble.

A masked man ran into a bank. Pointing his forefinger at the cashier he shouted out, 'Hand over the money. This is a muck up.' Coolly, the cashier replied, 'I think, Sir, you mean a hold up?'

'No. I mean a muck up. I left my gun in the car!'

To avoid mucking up your communications, spare the time for forethought and do not forget your notes, visual aids or other weapons.

At the start of your presentation, wait until you have the full, undivided and silent attention of your audience. Whether you are speaking to three, to thirty or three hundred, the principle is precisely the same. For your audience to pay attention to you, you must demand that attention from the start, nor must you start until you have that attention or you cannot hope to hold it. Method:

- Unless the Chair demands silence for you, stand – or, if necessary, sit – erect. Look your audience in the eye. Command silence with body language. Hold up one or both hands if necessary. Rap sharply on the table with a coin, or tap the side of a glass. A crisp sound draws attention.
- Wait for silence and attention and under no circumstances start talking until you get it.

Once under way, do not be afraid to pause.

16

The Art of the Pause

Communications, like meals, need digesting. Meals have courses; communications need staging. The more complex the subject, the greater the need for pause. The more brilliant the communicator, the harder it becomes to take breath.

My colleagues and I train executives in public speaking and presentational skills. We can change a lifetime of bad habit in two sessions, on consecutive days. The same process is not achievable by doubling the hours and cramming them into one day. Lessons sink into the psyche, during the pause, while the learner sleeps.

The pause is the top test of confidence – initially, apparent, and eventually, real – for any speaker. You wait until your audience is silent before you begin. You pause before key words and phrases, and especially as you build up to your climax. You recognize that you need time for yourself and for your audience, to take breath and thought.

We all recognize the human fountain gushes in a ceaseless flow on to an audience soon drenched in the spray of ideas. That was my style, when I began my apprenticeship in that debating society which is one of the toughest of all orator's training grounds, the Cambridge Union. It took three weeks of lessons, two hours a week day, with a remarkable teacher, to learn to throw my voice, my ideas and my message, with a variety of speed, mood and tone.

My tutor was skilled and bright. So why did it take him three weeks when we can usually achieve much the same results in two days? The answer lies in the magic of audio visual equipment. Listen to yourself, breathless, monotonous, unremitting. Watch yourself, as your eyes retreat to your notes, your speech incessant through fear of silence. Sound and pictures combine to teach more than any trainer.

Our victims take their video cassettes home. They can then play them, to the delight and laughter of their families. They can watch their own improvement, as the sessions proceed. No one can blackmail them with the horrors of their oratorical origins.

Not long ago, a television programme gave me their weekly political slot. I had fifteen minutes, all to myself. I was to prepare the script, turn up on location for the filming, do the interviewing and pass on my message.

I chose the topic – how not to be prosecuted for shoplifting when you are innocent. As I had been campaigning for years for change in both law and practice, I had no trouble with the script. The interviewing appeared to me to go well enough.

When the job was done, I asked the producer, who had been with me throughout and was an old Parliamentary colleague, who had lost his seat, 'How was it?'

'Good,' he replied. 'But you made two mistakes.'

'What were they?'

'When you were interviewing, you stood with your hands splendidly still – but clutched in front of you. You looked as if you were coming out of a public lavatory!'

Body language which was totally unintended. 'What to do?'

'Try perching on the edge of a table or bench. Relaxed.'

'The other error?'

'Much worse, for an interviewer. You asked questions and then did not give your interviewees time to answer. You were so afraid of silence on the air that you did not give your victim breathing time.'

So I had committed precisely that error against which I had long warned my distinguished pupils. Even on television, especially on the radio, and not only when on your feet – breathing time is time well allowed.

In my days as a barrister, I enjoyed that hunt which is cross-examination. As the witness began to crumble and the truth emerged, so I would increase the pace of the questioning.

The Judge, who was required to write down every important word in his notebook, would look up and say: 'Mr Janner. I suppose you don't want me to take down the witness's answers, do you?'

'Indeed, my Lord, I would be most grateful if you would do so.'

'In that case, Mr Janner,' said his Lordship, 'you must restrain your enthusiasm – and go much slower.'

I tried, and often failed. We all have our failings and that was mine. When I succeeded, the witness was then given time to think out the answer to the next question which I would probably ask. But in return, the Judge, the Magistrates or the jury had time to absorb the witness's last repy. It then became comparable with the next.

Patience and measured tread are not easy, with the eyes of your audience upon you. The more hostile their glare, the greater the difficulty, but the more worthwhile the art.

17

Taking Their Side

Sir Kenneth Cork was asked how to convince, to persuade, to avoid trouble. He replied, simply, 'Make them feel that you're on their side.'

That is a considerable problem if you are (as he explained) a company liquidator. It should be easier in most other communications.

If you are in the Chair, you should not usually take sides. But that does not mean that you have to be impartial as between the fire brigade and the fire. The meeting has put you into position so that you may ensure that the job is done, swiftly, efficiently and fairly. Your colleagues or the audience will accept your ruling if they believe that you are on the same side as they are – which means seeking the best results for the company, the organization, or the gathering.

If you are addressing the gathering, then start on the basis that each of your listeners must feel that you understand, appreciate and take fully into account their views, needs and aspirations. From that base, you can if necessary move into criticism, when it is more likely to be accepted.

For instance, explain why you are using a particular approach, and how it benefits your audience. I lecture on law. Sometimes, the subject has a certain inherent fascination; too often, it has great potential for boredom. So I enliven the proceedings by forcing the audience to answer questions; by teasing and taunting; by using anecdote and wit; and above all, by saying 'you' as often as possible – explaining to my listeners the personal relevance of the subject, the occasion, the rule.

I learned long ago that without explanation, people would say: 'He kept on picking on us . . . He wasted time with jokes . . . He could have packed in more information . . .'

So I tell them, 'You came here this morning expecting to be bored out of your minds, didn't you? You thought that you were going to be left alone, to sleep quietly in your seats, while I droned on at you about unfair dismissal, didn't you? Well, it's not going to be like that. I shall be asking you the questions because this subject is of crucial interest to you.'

Then we continue, 'I could drive you to distraction with great strings of legalisms – laws, statutes, regulations, cases. You would remember very few of them, and they are in your notes, anyway. What I shall do is give you a lucid summary of the essentials and show you how you can apply them so as to achieve your objects. If you have any questions at any time, indicate.'

In that way, we will all enjoy the day.

Communicating to employees? Then show that you understand their difficulties and are trying to find a solution that will satisfy them – for your benefit as well as theirs. You recognize the importance of satisfied colleagues.

Or perhaps you are selling goods or services? Far too many marketing people express their own wants and wishes, without placing nearly enough emphasis on the wishes of their prospects. You may give people the feeling that you are relating to them by talking in their language and from their aspect. Better still, listen. As so often, communication may be better achieved through the ears than by the mouth.

You know the signs over hospital beds: 'Nothing to be taken by mouth'? Try the communication alternative: 'Take only by ear'.

18

Take the Blame

There is no better way to create goodwill than to take the blame yourself. You probably deserve it.

If you allow a questioner, colleague, delegate or interviewee to wriggle off the hook of his or her own foolish question, you will earn appreciation. Conversely, you humiliate others at your own risk.

If the questions come from your superiors or from people with power over your future or that of your proposal, then it will scarcely help to compound the foolishness by slapping them down. Revenge will be theirs.

It is even more unforgivable to humiliate a subordinate, other than deliberately and as a deserved disciplinary rebuke, delivered in private. Do so before others and you will not be forgiven.

Now suppose that you apologize. You have nothing to lose but your words. Are you so sure that the stupid question would have been asked had you given adequate information to your audience? The following are tried and unbeatable routes to appreciation:

- I am so sorry, I should have explained that point. . . .
- My apologies. I obviously did not make the situation clear. . . .
- I am so sorry. I should have recognized my professional jargon and explained the problem more clearly. . . .
- My fault. I should have expanded on that point before. . . .
- Thank you for that question. It shows that I did not make the situation sufficiently clear. Let me try again. . . .
- That's a very important question and one that I should have dealt with in my introduction/address. Let me make up for the omission now. . . .
- Thank you for that question. It emphasizes the point I was making that . . . and gives me the chance to expand on it. . . .

A sign of true statesmanship is, though, the apology unwarranted.

The ten-year-old son of American friends of mine lost an arm in an accident. To cheer him up, the then Secretary of State, Dean Acheson, invited him to lunch at the State Department. The waiter served up steak.

The boy stared miserably at his plate. How could he cut his meat, with one hand? But, how could he ask anyone so mighty to cut the steak for him?

When he arrived home that evening, his parents asked him, 'How was it?' He told them about the steak.

'So what happened?'

'A miracle,' he replied. 'Mr Acheson said to me, "I'm so sorry, but I wonder whether you'd do me a favour. The waiter has given you the steak cooked as I like it – and I've got yours. Would you mind swapping?" "Of course not," I answered. So we swapped plates.'

'So what was the miracle?' asked his father.

'Mr Acheson had already cut his up, before I got it!'

Now transfer this marvellous technique of swapping the miseries to the ordinary routine of the presentation or interview.

Someone asked a query? Do not exclaim your disbelief: 'How could someone in your position ask such a question?'

A questioner shows that his mind has been wandering while you were explaining. Do not retort: 'Sir, if you kept your ears as open as your mouth, you would learn more.'

The fact that everyone else in the audience thinks that the question is unnecessary, stupid, repetitive or plain ignorant will do you no harm. The more unnecessary, stupid, repetitive or ignorant the query, the greater the appreciation for your answer.

Appreciation from the questioner, of course. He or she will almost certainly recognize where the error lay and appreciate your tact. The greater the recognized stupidity, repetitiveness or ignorance, the more profound the questioner's appreciation – which may be shown in due course by giving you the job, the contract, the favour or whatever else it is that you seek.

As for the rest of the audience, you will have their appreciation too. They will recognize and salute your tact. If they put that recognition into practical form, you will have deserved the accolade of success.

19

The Psychology of the Moment

Before you make any presentation, ask yourself four questions:
- Who are my audience? That includes: how many?
- What do they want from me? Incorporating: why are they here?
- What is my message? In other words: what do I want to convey? why am I here?
- How do I get my message across?

Too many communicators begin with question four. Without the others, it is impossible to answer, because you cannot succeed without taking the psychology of the people and of the occasion fully into account.

Actors have no alternative other than to put across their scripted material, irrespective of the audience who happen to turn up. Even then, they will tell you that precisely the same words are spoken to the same number of people in the same place in (generally) an identical way, will produce wildly varying results. Audiences, like individuals, have moods. Those with moods suffer also from mood swings.

So when you are preparing a presentation, pause, think, ask yourself the four questions, then reflect on the psychology which is most likely to get your message across.

Maybe you are in what is irreverently termed a 'beauty contest', pitching against other companies or firms. Before you decide who is going to make the presentation and how, you must ask your four questions and then the fifth: what is the psychology of the moment?

Suppose that you want to achieve some particular result on a one to one basis. Do you charm, cajole, and flatter? Or should you be firm, unyielding, and hard? Or perhaps you should bring a colleague so that one of you takes the soft line, the other the hard?

Whatever you decide, allow yourself to react to the atmosphere of the moment. The reason why it is generally a disaster to write out your speeches or presentations, word for word, is that you lose that flexibility which results from reaction to your audience. You must keep constant eye contact, so as to watch for that reaction.

Still, you should combine your experience and, if necessary, that of colleagues, in a conscious attempt to assess in advance the psychology of the moment. The preparation of communications deserves far more time, thought and attention than it usually gets. It is needed by the inexperienced, of course. But too many senior and accomplished people allow overconfidence to result in under preparation – especially in that unrecognized essential, the psychology of the moment.

20

Sensitivity, Tact, Humour and Flattery

As a radio only performs well if properly tuned in to the station, so you cannot captivate your audience without tuning in to their sensitivities. You must watch your audience with care; coax them into concentration; convince them with your theme; enthuse them with your message; involve them and their interests in your words; and by watching and listening to their reactions and paying heed to their interests, you will communicate properly with them, whether you are making the speech or listening to theirs.

Sensitivity will guide you to the top person, to accord appropriate greeting, respect and if necessary, a touch of flattery. It will help you to steer the conversation, discussion or presentation in the direction that you wish. You will be ready to invite audience intervention or participation and to make the best of it.

Sensitivity means avoiding jargon where possible and explaining it where necessary. Do not presume that others have specialized knowledge which you could expect of them – but take care never to talk down.

If a gentleman is one who never unintentionally offends, sharpened sensitivity will guide your intent. It will ensure that you use humour without malice or insult and tact without the appearance of insincerity.

Flattery means telling others what they would like to think of themselves. It is a major weapon, crucial to the answer or deflecting of questions, to the selling of ideas or of products, to successful communication.

Communication through humour is an art of its own. Amateurs fear it without due cause. Professionals grant it insufficient respect.

Take your friend who is a joy by the table or bar, a raconteur who delights his audience. Put him on his feet after dinner and as like as not he will dry up. Why? Because he has not learned to transfer the same style and relaxation to the apparently formal and upright as he does to the private and relaxed. Believe in your humour. Be prepared to shrug if a joke goes adrift. Tell jokes against yourself and your own country, race or religion and be vastly careful not to offend by telling stories that could cause hurt to others. And breed confidence through preparation and practice.

The tasteless joke is death. I once saw the magnificent Danny Kaye 'die' on stage, at a Royal Command Performance. The Queen was in the Royal Box and did not laugh at his sally at the Royal Family.

Industrial leaders have been forced into resignation by racist jokes, told in private, but repeated in public. Political leaders have been forced to apologize – remember Nicholas Ridley and his unseemly jest about open doors, after the Zeebrugge ferry disaster?

Humour is an invaluable ally to the skilled communicator. But like all other weapons, it requires care, practice and humility in its use.

21

Trust and Sincerity

As with the words, so with the voice – low key is usually best. Writer Lilian Hellman remarked: 'The English don't raise their voices, although they may have other vulgarities.' Albion is more visibly perfidious when she shouts.

The higher the voice, the smaller the intellect and the lesser the impact. Or as an opera fan once said: 'If anything is too silly to say, you can always sing it.' And, of course, the bigger the lie, the louder and more often it gets shouted.

Most people enjoy the music of their own voices. Good communicators turn down the volume and adjust the tone. The greater the call for sincerity and trust, the more subtle the sound should be.

In great, past generations of legal advocates – the era of Clarence Darrow in the United States and F. E. Smith (Lord Birkenhead) in Britain – the florid oration and especially the melodramatic address to the jury were standard fare. Today is the time of the more gentle and sincere approach, the cajoling of the mind, perfected by the great Lord Birkett.

An American politician was once asked how you could tell when President Richard Nixon was telling the truth. 'When he clenches his fists and shakes them,' he replied, 'you know that the President is telling the truth. When he holds up his hands to the skies and twists his chin as he speaks, you know that he is telling the truth. But when he opens his mouth . . .'

In his acceptance speech, President Nixon said: 'Let us begin by committing ourselves to the truth, to see it like it is and to tell it like it is, to find the truth, to speak the truth and live with the truth. That's what we'll do.'

Loud cheers for Watergate. The man was much more believable when (as reported in official Minutes of a White House meeting) he referred to his administration as having 'the first complete, far reaching attack on the problem of hunger in history.' How to do it?

'We use all the rhetoric, so long as it doesn't cost money,' said the President.

Brevity and the soft word are the sisters of trust and sincerity.

22

Name Them!

To communicate with or about an individual human being, use a name. Get it right. The sound of your own name is sweet music. But no note is more discordant than a mispronunciation, misuse or mistake.

Names matter. Few insults are more degrading than removing people's names. Prisoners and convicts are not known by numbers merely for administrative convenience. It is an unworthy part of the dehumanizing process that takes away the individuality of those locked up.

When the Nazis herded their victims into Auschwitz, that most foul of extermination camps, guards shaved their heads and tattooed numbers onto their forearms. Jews, gypsies, dissenters, trade unionists and the rest were sub-humans. The shaven head and the numbered arm were signals of death and despair, to the inmates and to those who guarded them.

The best gifts that parents can give newborn children are names that they will live with in peace and appreciation. The best compliment that others can later pay is to use and to pronounce those names, often and correctly.

Shakespeare asked, 'What's in a name? That which we call a rose, by any other name would smell as sweet'. Which may have been good enough for Romeo or for Juliet, but it will not do with ordinary mortals with whom you wish to communicate on loving, affectionate, friendly or even courteous terms.

We treasure our good names. 'Who steals my purse steals trash', said Othello. ' 'Tis something, nothing; 'Twas mine, 'tis his, and has been slave to thousands. But he that filches from me my good name, robs me of that which not enriches him, and makes me poor indeed.'

In the 1970 General Election, the Chair of a Women's Conservative Rally delighted the nation, watching on TV. Introducing Party Leader, Edward Heath, she proclaimed 'And now, ladies, it is my pleasure to introduce to you . . . a man whose name is a household word . . . our next Prime Minister . . . Mr . . . er . . . er . . . er . . !'

The unfortunate woman had forgotten the basic rule of all introductions. Write the name of the guest or other person to be introduced in large letters on your notes. Under the stress of any great moment and of many minor ones, the most precise mind may forget the most beloved and familiar name.

Introducing colleagues to a guest of honour, put their names onto a card and carry it in your hand. Once the writing is there, you will almost certainly not need to refer to it. If you have no available reminder, then panic may erase names and atrophy the mind.

The Royal Family is brilliant in its memory for names and occasions. This flattering skill is partly the result of training and experience, partly of careful briefing. 'Fancy the Duke of Edinburgh remembering me, after all this time . . . .'

'Wasn't it wonderful that Princess Diana remembered our function at Hampton Court. . . .' Names and occasions remembered are friendships and loyalties affirmed.

How can ordinary mortals, with miserable memories or inadequate briefings cope with names? The mind can be trained.

My friend, David Berglas – brilliant magician and master of the mind – teaches memory for names. Briefly: you associate the name with a way-out word; you repeat both, often and clearly; and remember that the mind is an infinitely expandable container which operates better and not worse because its proprietor programmes more information, not less.

Before you write or memorize the name, check on the spelling or pronunciation (respectively). If you introduce guests whose names may be pronounced in various ways, enquire, 'Forgive me, but how is your name correctly pronounced?' No one minds being asked for the correct pronunciation, but everyone objects to errors in naming.

Parliamentary rules on 'naming' are quaint. The Speaker refers to Members by their names, but the Members are not permitted to do so. They are, 'My Honourable Friend, the Member for Leicester West' or 'The Right Honourable Lady, the Prime Minister'. MPs do not speak in the House or to each other in their personal capacities. We are the elected representatives of our constituencies.

There is always much merriment when the Speaker forgets or mispronounces a Member's name or, better still, calls on a Member by someone else's. Speakers seldom fail from time to time to do so. They are forgiven. Others are not.

The Speaker's ultimate weapon is to 'name' a recalcitrant MP, generally one who makes an improper allegation against a colleague and refuses to withdraw it on the Speaker's instructions or who otherwise refuses to obey the Speaker's ruling. The 'named' person must leave the Chamber.

At least in the House both the Speaker and the miscreant communicate clearly one to the other, by name known to both. The same does not apply when hotels, airlines and others attempt to make contact or to page someone with names like mine. If I book a room at a hotel and no reservation is recorded, I invite them to look under 'Tanner', 'Jenner' or 'James'.

As my late father was a Life Peer, I enjoy (if that be the correct word) the courtesy title of 'Honourable'. Many missing reservations have been traced under 'Honourable Janner' – and not in Japan, either. Other successful efforts to trace me have included: 'Reverend Banner', 'General Tanner' and 'MP Jackson'.

Anyway, if you wish to address, introduce or communicate with someone whose name is only a household word in his own household, please take care how you do it. Only his sense of humour can turn your error away from ill-will and into laughter.

23

The Courtesy of a Reply

If you receive a communication which you dislike, you have two possible retorts: the first, a reply; the second, no reply. Your choice will depend on your situation.

Your reply may be direct or indirect. You may answer the other person by letter, telephone or personal meeting. Consider each possibility with care:

- Use the written response when you need to put your reply firmly on the record. But prepare with care and recognize that any mistake will be held against you. A word on paper is worth ten by mouth – provided that the words are precise.
- The telephone is useful, for swift reply. Much nastiness has been diffused by swift conversation, 'I am so sorry about the misunderstanding . . . obviously we got this wrong . . . I've read your letter and I apologize that I did not make myself clear. My fault, I'm sure. . . .'

  But the telephone is no place for a row. Unless you intend to be apologetic and not apoplectic, cool down and put a draft onto paper.

  Nor should you reckon that your telephone call will necessarily go unrecorded. Those who monitor messages from the moon have no difficulty in recording a chat by phone.
- Eyeball to eyeball is generally best. Meet – perhaps on mutual ground and when and where relaxed. It is usually harder to be nasty in person when you are relaxed.

Sometimes, though, it is better to stay silent. The words will not be wrong and the silence is itself a communication. It may also have other advantages:

- If the communicator fails to draw response or blood, he may get bored with the battle, or simply forget it.

- If there really is no answer to give and you are not prepared to withdraw or to apologize, then you are better off to give none.
- If a response would only make matters worse, by it contributing to a worsening of relations with those with whom you would or should improve them – then shut up. And cover up . . . close down communication, if only for the moment, then hope for the best.

Whenever I get a really nasty letter in my mail which, regrettably, is not infrequent, I work out the best response. If the letter is filthy or fascist or both, then it gets consigned to the appropriate file. But if the correspondent has mellowed vitriol with courtesy, I always reply.

'I am sure that you did not intend your letter to be as personally offensive as it read, so I am taking the trouble of replying to the specific points that you raise.' Nine times out of ten, the correspondent writes again. 'Thank you for your letter. I am glad that you did not take offence, when none was intended. Clearly, we disagree on the issues, but at least I now know the basis for your views.'

This also provides a marvellous response, when you do not agree and are bound to say so. Other alternatives:

- 'You are, of course, entitled to your point of view. I am sorry that I cannot agree with it, but. . . .'
- 'It is good that in this country we can disagree without being disagreeable! I did appreciate your writing to me . . . .'
- 'One joy of living in a democratic country is that each of us is entitled to be wrong! In this case, I believe that you are because. . . .'

Anyway, if you are in doubt as to whether or not silence is the best answer, keep it. With rare exceptions, it is better to bite your tongue before you have spoken.

Use charm, if you can. That (said Albert Camus) is 'a way of getting the answer "yes" without having asked any clear questions'. It is also the way to avoid getting the answer 'no', without putting your views into the wrong words.

As Camus again said, with such truth, 'Men are never convinced of your reasons, of your sincerity, of the seriousness of your suffering, except by your death.' So just accept that the choice is between getting something wrong through speech or through silence, your chances of convincing the opposition may be better by taking breath than by using it.

Finally: please do not think that silence as a response is a passive retort. The Gandhian doctrines of 'Satyatgraha' and of 'ahimsa' – of passive resistance and of self restraint – changed the face of a continent. There is even an aggression, inherent in active passivity.

Conversely: if you reply in words or, more precisely and permanently, by letter or other document, then make sure that you get your strategy and your tactics in proper order. As Abba Eban pointed out in his brilliant book, *The New Diplomacy*, 'One can make an omelette out of eggs but nobody has ever reconstructed eggs out of an omelette.' Or in the less witty but equally pungent words of Omar Khayyam, 'The moving finger writes and having writ moves on. Nor all thy piety nor wit shall lure it back to cancel half a line, nor all thy tears wash out a word of it.'

24

Non-communication

Silence is a golden art. To describe someone as 'non-communicative' is only a compliment when you are praising discretion. To be non-communicative may present special problems.

Bad news broke while my wife, Myra, and I were abroad at a conference. The day we returned home, the telephone rang. Myra answered. 'This is the *Sunday Express*,' said the voice. 'Can I speak to Mr Janner?'

'I'm afraid he's away,' she said.

'Then who are you, please?'

'I'm looking after the house while the Janners are away,' said my wife.

'When are you expecting them back?'

'I'm so sorry,' said Myra, her tongue firmly embedded in her cheek, 'but I don't know.' The reporter rang off.

The following day, the reporter phoned again. 'Are you the lady looking after the house for the Janners?' he asked.

'Yes,' said Myra.

'Are the Janners back?' he asked.

'No, I'm afraid they're not,' said Myra.

'Well, I thought that I should tell you that you are wrong,' said the reporter. 'I thought you might like to know that they have returned to England.'

'Really?' said Myra. 'Where are they?'

'They're in Leicester,' said the reporter, in a tone of deep confidence. 'They're in Mr Janner's constituency. . . .'

My wife thanked him and I congratulated her on a job well done.

The greater your problem, the more difficult it becomes to avoid publicity. It is, after all, the job of the media to produce stories. If you are in the public eye, you must expect it to glare at you. If it invades your home, you are entitled to blind it.

These tactics should be sparingly used. The best way to win trust from the press is to share trust with it. Make it absolutely plain that you are speaking 'off the record' and the chances of your confidence being breached are remote. In a quarter century of public life, no media representative has ever dishonoured an 'off the record' confidence that I placed in him or her.

Once you have unburdened yourself 'off the record', the journalist may reasonably try to get at least part of your statement firmly onto it. 'Can I report that you . . . surely I could tell our readers that you . . .'

It is the journalist's job to produce copy. Consider in each case whether it may not be better to provide it, in the friendliest form you can achieve, rather than possibly appearing shifty and secretive, as revealed by that telling phrase, 'Mr Brown refused to comment'. Or, 'Although this programme spoke several times to Miss Smith, she declined to put her case'.

So before you non-communicate, consider: might it not be better to put your version on the record? And if, after consideration, you decide that silence is the best answer, then consider with care how best to achieve it.

How many of your colleagues are holding back information from their immediate subordinates, in case their own positions may be at risk? Or is it only in other peoples' businesses that units are so competitive that they would even prefer to do business with or even to give advantages or information to competitors, in preference to their own colleagues?

That delightful and witty writer and raconteur, Stephen Potter, created the international sport of 'Gamesmanship'. Its most important element 'one-upmanship'. Its essence: ensuring that you do not communicate to others that which you would be better off to keep for yourself.

Take your line management, for example. Already, they are probably disgruntled because at least some of the people whom they supervise earn more than they do. These junior or middle managers work 'such hours as may be necessary for the proper performance of their duties'. Which means: no overtime – and probably no bonus or commission either. In return for the great privilege of 'being part of our management team', they get paid less and are kept in the dark as much as possible.

The immortal description of this method of non-communication is, of course, 'mushroom' or 'seagull' management. The boss birds fly briefly overhead; fertilise the soil beneath with their droppings, and soar back into the night.

How, then, can and do these subordinates get their revenge? They have two main methods:

- They get the information from other sources. These include: bright eyed office staff, and trade union luminaries.
- Information once acquired, they either keep it to themselves and use it to protect their own backs, or share it only with those whom they regard as their own colleagues – which means: people at their own level and below and certainly not those who bomb them from above.

Office staff? Of course. There are no secrets from the secretaries, the computer operators, the recorders and the filers of confidential information.

Union officials? Unlike managers, convenors or even stewards have direct access to the managing director or even the chairman, and are often on first name terms with him. They then get the information and (assuming that they themselves are not part of the conspiracy of deliberate silence), will pass it back to the personnel or other manager with whom they have established a relationship of decent trust.

In the UK, we are drifting away from 'personnel' into the Americanized glory of 'human resources'. The greatest resource of human beings is the information locked up in their heads. Its extraction should be the manager's top task.

Or consider that the only partially true but ever hopeful management cliché, 'You are all a part of the business . . . we are all in the same team . . . we share the same purpose. . . .'

In reality just as the individual interests of the Board are often totally different from those of the shareholders, so management, in the purported interests of shareholders spends too much time plotting against the work force.

That does not just mean 'avoiding excessive wage demands', and making low or 'lower' pay acceptable to the troops. It also involves the withholding of information in good times and thrusting it forward only when it will not encourage employees or their representatives to claim too much.

It is customary at Jewish prayers in memory of a departed person for someone to say at least a few words of praise, by way of farewell. At one such gathering, the Rabbi declined the duty and honour for himself. He later told his wife, he could not really find anything good to say about the deceased.

'Now then,' he enquired of the mourners, 'who will say something about our departed brother, David?' Silence.

'Please,' he replied, 'Won't one of you declaim the good in him?'

Silence. Then a man spoke from the back, 'I've got something to say,' he pronounced, humbly. 'His brother was worse!'

In the theory of commerce, not least in the sphere of personnel or human resources, a communication is accepted as a necessity. In reality, withholding the information may be bad. To communicate (they think) could be worse.

One final example. In Peking (or Beijing, as it is now properly known), we once asked the then British Ambassador 'Why is it that the Japanese are so much more likely to get contracts than we are? Is it simply because they are nearer and have a better understanding of the oriental mind?'

'Not at all,' he replied, without hesitation. 'Our team will come over here in a delegation from a Chamber of Commerce. They won't stay long enough. They are limited in their patience, while the Japanese will sit it out until they get what they came for.

'What's more our characters will be competing with each other. They will be selling the same or similar goods. Naturally, they won't share their expertise, their information or their knowledge. The Japanese, on the other hand, will send a complementary team, each pushing related but not competing goods. And they pool their information. So they win.'

In the long run, communication means success. Non-communication – by habit or by deliberation – creates barriers between colleagues, at every level. Between nations and businesses, it contains the seeds of conflict. Communication may sometimes do harm. But its silent, non-communicating brother is nearly always much worse.

25

Ten Ways Not to Answer

Ordinarily, you should always seek to answer fully any questions posed by employees, customers or colleagues, if you are to be a good communicator. Rarely, however, you may be faced with a question which it is impossible, for whatever reason, for you to answer. In such a case you must be able to avoid humiliation when evading the question.

Here's a list of ways to avoid directly answering an unwanted question without seeming rude:

1 Come clean and say that you do not know the answer. Followed by:
   - 'But I'll find out for you and let you know . . .'
   - 'It's a very good question. I wonder if any of you can answer it?'
   - 'But it's not really relevant . . .'
   - 'I'll get one of my colleagues to find the answer for you and will let you know.'

2 Say, 'That's an important question and I'm coming to that problem very shortly . . . in the next part of my lecture . . . tomorrow morning . . .' You then have two alternatives. You can and should 'come to it' – but you may not, in which case you must hope that your questioner will forget.

3 Say, 'Now, that's an interesting one. Do any of you know the answer?' With any luck, somebody will. If you are unlucky and nobody does, then you can revert to 1 above.

4 Throw the answer back at the questioner. 'What do you think? I expect you know the answer to that one yourself, don't you? Well, how would you put it?'

5 Answer a different question. This is typical of Ministerial answers to MPs. By all means supply information which you hope will satisfy the questioner. But you avoid giving information which you either do not know or which you do not want to reveal.

6   Refuse to answer. You will normally have to give some at least apparently acceptable reason, for instance:
  - 'I'm sorry, but to answer that question would involve breach of confidence . . .'
  - 'Unfortunately, that is information which is really not mine to give. Would you perhaps like to have a word with . . . who may be prepared to say more than I can . . .'
  - 'I have answered this question very fully already. I am not prepared to discuss this matter any further.'

7   Request that the question be discussed privately. Try the following:
  - 'That is a very important question, but it really is one that is particular to you and to your business. Would you be kind enough to have a word with me afterwards and I will try to answer it for you?'
  - 'I am so sorry, but I have so little time left to complete this presentation. Would you mind discussing this problem with us, over lunch?'

8   Referring the queston to a committee (see also Chapter 25). Thus:
  - 'This is a very complex question. I am going to ask Roger, Mary and Bill to be good enough to meet and to discuss it and then to report back to us.'
  - 'Let's set up a sub-committee to look into that question. It is really unsuitable for a gathering of this size. We need some serious research, don't we?'
  - 'I really can't answer this question when it is one which comes within the ambit of our PR Committee. But I will undertake to pass it on to its Chairman and ask them to provide us with a view.'

9   Provide an apparent answer. Do so in a way that sounds plausible and real, and hope that the listeners will not recognize it as a non-answer. This may work, especially, if you can:

10 Deflect attention. This is the magician's technique of mis-direction. You look at the right hand while the left deposits the rabbit in the hat. Thus: instead of answering the question, you draw attention to whatever diversion comes to mind. Maybe:
  - 'Ah, yes, Mr. Brown. It is very good to hear from you. We do congratulate you on the results of your department. What tremendous advances you have made. Now, I have been meaning to enquire whether you need further resources in order to achieve . . .'

- 'Yes. An important question – and one that the Chancellor of the Exchequer would dearly like to answer. Did you see him on television last night? I wonder what you thought of his approach to our industry, our problems, our future . . . ?'

For the avoidance of doubt, questions should where possible be answered – briskly, briefly, satisfactorily and without disrupting your argument or the structure of your presentation. The above techniques are for those occasional but inevitable exceptions.

26

Refusals

There is an art to communicating a refusal, whether or not you wish to offend the invitor. You could simply bin the offer. Silence is often the ultimate insult. But if you do reply, how should you communicate your regrets?

The famous American General, William Sherman, received a message from the Republican Convention. Would he be their Presidential candidate? He wired back, 'If nominated, I will not accept. If elected, I will not serve.' At least his reply left no one in any doubt.

Richard Porson, a famous British classical scholar in the late eighteenth century, was renowned for the rudeness of his retorts. Invited to express his opinion of contemporary poet, Robert Southey, he replied to him personally, 'Your works will be read after Shakespeare and Milton are forgotten. And not until then.' When invited to dinner by a distinguished poet, Samuel Rogers, he replied, 'Thank you, no. I dined yesterday.'

Enough nastiness. How do you communicate regret that is well felt?

You could start with what Disraeli called his 'Series of Congratulatory Regrets'. Circumscribe your apology with praise. Tell your would-be hosts how much you appreciate the excellence and importance of their work, their project, their organization. But do not overfill your ladle or you invite the rejoinder, 'If we are as wonderful as you say, then surely you could spare us a moment of your own time?' Balance should be your aim.

Second: if you have a genuine and acceptable reason, then give it. If, for instance, you are genuinely presiding over or addressing another gathering at that time, or if you will be abroad, on business or even away on holiday, then say so. But it is as dangerous to identify a previous engagement which you have just decided to acquire as it would be to respond by saying that you confidently expect to be unwell on the date in question.

If you really would like to be asked again, then write, 'I am immensely sorry that I cannot accept your invitation. But I appreciated receiving it; I would so much have liked to be with you; and I do hope that you will ask me again.'

Do avoid that ploy, if you would prefer to be left alone. It was said of one persistent refuser, 'He keeps assuring us that he wants to come and asking us to present his deep regrets to the gathering, but every time he gets asked, he refuses.'

So what are the best, standard refusals, non-commital and inoffensive?

If the date is too near, you have no problem. 'I am so sorry that I cannot avoid a previous and long-standing commitment.' If, but only if, you would like to be asked again, add, 'I do hope that on some future occasion, you will be kind enough to give me much more notice. Perhaps we could even put our diaries together and find a mutually convenient date.'

If the date is deliberately far ahead, so as to make sure that you have no previous commitments, the problem gets tougher. 'Please do choose any weekday to suit yourself, perhaps in the spring of next year.'

Reply, 'I am so sorry, but it is impossible for me to know at this stage what my commitments will be, so far ahead.' If (but again, only if) you would like to be reinvited, say, 'Perhaps you would contact me again nearer the date and I will do my best to come.' Or even, 'I have pencilled the date into my diary and I do hope to be with you. But perhaps your secretary would check with mine, two or three months before the date?'

If the date is left entirely open, you have only one last refuge – the truth. 'I have so many business and public commitments in my diary that I really cannot take on any more within the foreseeable future. I am so sorry to have to disappoint you and I hope you will understand, but much as I would like to come to your organization, it is simply impossible for me to do so.'

If you receive a personal letter, then it deserves a reply, signed by you. If it is a standard, printed card, then you can properly use a standard reply, sent by your secretary. 'Mr Jones regrets that he will be unable to attend your gathering/reception/dinner, due to a previous engagement. Please do accept and present his apologies. He has asked me to say how much he hopes that your gathering/reception/dinner will be a great success.'

If you wish to combine your absence with a touch of upstaging, you could (if appropriate) donate a prize or a presentation, or arrange for a generous personal or company donation to the cause. Your token of regret will be real, tangible, appreciated and duly recorded.

Or you could offer an acceptable substitute, as guest or as speaker. But do make sure that your offer will not itself offend.

Finally, I like the sad communication, sent by an employee to his firm, during a traffic crisis. 'Regret cannot come today; have not yet got home yesterday!'

27

Misunderstandings

Curious to know how a prospective assistant had come to apply for my job, I asked him at the end of his interview: 'How did you find me?'

'Absolutely charming!' he replied.

Which may not have provided the information I sought, but which reminded me of the American job applicant who, when I asked him whether he had any questions for me, replied, 'Does it help you in politics that you were a tennis champion?'

I was once an excellent sprinter – an attribute of some help to any politician. But tennis? Never.

'Where did you get the idea that I played tennis?' I asked.

'I looked you up in *Who's Who*, and it said that in 1955 you contested Wimbledon!'

I had indeed stood as Labour candidate for that illustrious seat, where I was defeated by a mere 12,000 votes. That was the nearest I had got to tennis.

This sort of merry misunderstanding adds spice to the interview. But important lack of understanding poisons the process before it begins.

Since the days of the Romans, the basis of any contract is that the party should be 'ad idem' – that their minds should be as one. If the main terms of any deal are not agreed, it will generally be unenforceable. Agreement requires understanding.

If one party or the other enters into a contract by mistake, then that may be his or her misfortune. The battles of mistaken litigants fill both law reports and lawyers' pockets.

In commerce, errors due to misunderstanding are the source of unnecessary loss, irritation and law suits. Where the contract involves employment – the employee's livelihood and the employer's good management and industrial relations – then clarity and precision are the parents of understanding and the avoidance of suffering, personal and financial.

The process begins with the advertisement. Let prospective applicants or customers know what you seek and fewer will waste your time and their own by offering to buy or sell unwanted services. Conversely, if you save money by carefully curtailing your advert, you will almost certainly lose far more through unnecessary interviews.

In March 1986, King Juan Carlos and Queen Sofia of Spain paid an official state visit to Britain. Interspersed into its series of glittering and joyful occasions was a series of actual and potential misunderstandings. The first two were the product of an otherwise relaxed and excellent BBC radio interview, carried out by the King in his accented but fluent English.

Asked about his forthcoming address to both Houses of Parliament in the Royal Gallery, the King expressed his delight and appreciation. 'I am grateful to Her Majesty's Government for this great privilege,' he said.

The King could not have been the first monarch to address both Houses, without the unanimous consent of all political parties. The Government received him officially but the Opposition was equally to be thanked. To avoid that sort of misunderstanding, you must know the subtleties of the system. Overseas customs, curious and arcane, need careful checking.

This unwitting error of courtesy was pointed out to His Majesty, who did not repeat it in his dignified Parliamentary address. I hope that he was also told that when MPs growl in unison, that is a sign of appreciation.

Introducing the King, the Lord Chancellor, robed in all the glory of a Gilbert and Sullivan production, backed by the Yeomen of the Guard in their Tudor uniforms, rightly praised the King for his courage in preserving democracy in Spain. The audience erupted, united in a deep throated roar. The initiated would have recognized this as the height of Parliamentary approval. To those who know it not, it could signify the cannibal's pre-breakfast rumble.

The top error of the visit, though, was produced by the press. The King (we were told) was on his way to Oxford University, 'to receive a doctorate in civil war'! The joke was spoiled when a terrorist bomb killed eight innocent shoppers in Madrid that morning. The intent of those murderers was well understood, in Spain and in Britain alike.

28

Handling Confrontation

If your communication is well and quietly received, then you are fortunate. Next time, you may not be.

So consider: if you are confronted with a confrontation, how do you handle it? If you are attacked by those whom you need on your side, how can you deflect the onslaught, make the interrogator your ally, your client, your customer? How does the professional presenter deal with the skilled confronter?

You start by recognizing the reality. In his classic fudge at the time of the Suez campaign, Prime Minister Anthony Eden (later Lord Avon) informed the House of Commons, 'We are not at war with Egypt. We are in an unarmed conflict.' Question for you: are you the victim of true aggression, or simply being tested or teased? Assess your questioner before you react.

If in doubt, you could hedge, perhaps with a smile. Another Eden classic: when a reporter asked him, 'What will be the effect on international affairs if Stalin dies?', he replied, 'That is a good question for you to ask, but not a wise question for me to answer!'

If you need time to think, though, do not repeat the question. Thus:

'Why is your charge so heavy? Why is it higher than your competitors?'

If you reply, 'Why are our charges so heavy? Why are they more than our competitors?' that is a horror. Try instead, 'I'll tell you why . . .' or 'That's a fair question. Let me explain. . . .'

If (but only if) the question is either unclear or capable of misinterpretation, ask for it to be repeated. 'I'm sorry. I didn't catch the question.' Or, 'It's my fault, I'm sure – but are you asking if . . . or whether . . .?'

Next, and always: keep your cool. If you lose it, you are done for. Anger is a brief madness which should only be feigned.

Bernard Shaw once said, 'If you strike a child, take care that you strike it in anger, even at the risk of maiming its life. A blow in cold blood neither can nor should be forgiven.'

In adult controversy, the rule is the opposite. If you strike out in retaliation at a questioner, take care that you do so in cold blood. If you counter-attack in anger, you will main your argument for ever and will seldom be forgiven.

Lose control of yourself and of your tongue, then, and at the same moment you also lose control of the argument.

If you are interrupted in mid-flow, have the confidence to pause. Either allow your interrogater to continue or say, with courteous calm, 'Please let me finish my answer.'

If faced with aggression, follow the principles of any good psychiatrist or social worker. React gently. If you counter with aggression, you will simply feed the fires of ill will. Which is a pity, if your antagonist is trying to stoke you up in order to do you harm. It is even more so if they are merely testing your mettle. You need a cool mind to deflect heat.

If the other party is sufficiently determined to attack you, you may eventually decide to use some well known diplomatic techniques. These you may delegate to the staff of your mission, at whatever level; or you may feel that a word from you now may save many in the future. Either way, here are some useful possibilities, well known to our missions abroad.

First: time. Try the following sample code phrases:

'It's not the right moment, is it?'

'I shall be glad to look into this, in due course.'

'It shouldn't be long before we can usefully discuss the matter. I'll be in touch.'

'We don't consider that progress can be made until. . . .'

'Yes, I am looking forward to a chat with you about . . . I am only sorry that we are still waiting for . . . and until then, it really would be a waste of both our time.'

'I am so sorry. I really must insist that we postpone our meeting until . . . . Then let's have a chat over a drink, shall we? Or maybe we could meet over lunch? Or I would be very glad to welcome you as my guest to . . . and we can put our heads together about it.'

All politicians are familiar with governmental 'urgency'. Indeed, that most genial and witty of peers, former Lord Chancellor Elwyn Jones, has described the word 'urgent' in those circumstances as 'what we all recognize as code for never!'

For instance, it was alleged that some 17 Nazi war criminals had entered and were probably still living in the United Kingdom. In October 1986, I wrote to Prime Minister Margaret Thatcher, asking for an investigation. I received an immediate reply saying that the matter was being investigated 'urgently'. It was February 1987 before Downing Street laboured and gave birth to a Ministerial mouse, namely the reply that, regrettably, nothing could be done. (In fact a top-level enquiry was subsequently set up.)

Note, though, that the Prime Minister gave her promise of 'urgent attention' without delay. The more promptly you communicate your good intentions, the more likely it becomes that your adversary will accept them at their face value and forgive your transmissions, or the lack thereof. A second technique is to refer the matter to a committee, by whatever name. If you wish to keep your communicant at bay, the status quo in position, then a committee (in whatever guise) is an ideal instrument. Thus:

> 'A great idea. Let's get Joe, Bill and Mary to look into it, shall we? They can report back urgently' (Once again, that's the key word.)

> 'I'm so sorry not to have been able to get in touch with you earlier. Like you, I am absolutely drowned with work. But I do agree that we must make swift progress now. So let's delegate the next stage to . . .' (Delegations attend conferences, which are themselves carefully designed to avoid concrete results.) 'What matters,' you will be told, 'is that we are still talking.' Or, in the words of former Prime Minister, James Callaghan: 'Jaw, jaw, not war, war'.

A skilled observer at a recent conference concerning the future of Gibraltar and attended by distinguished delegations, led by the foreign ministers of Britain and Spain and the Chief Minister of Gibraltar, summed up its 'success' thus: 'In the course of time, conversations like this will build up mutual confidence and goodwill and enable progress to be made on the substantive matters.'

In other words, we have no intention whatever of (in the case of the British) discussing and (in that of the Spaniards) not discussing, Spanish sovereignty over the Rock; and therefore we must keep our communications (including the frontier post at La Linea) open, by continuing to have delegations conferring at conferences. Meanwhile, perhaps someone will dream up a formula.

Communication techniques, then, need formulas. You may create one yourself or delegate the job to a delegation (which you may call a committee), which will meet with those on the other side to confer at a conference and (you never know, do you?) perhaps a 'mutually acceptable solution' may be found. If not, then at least you have avoided 'unnecessary confrontation'.

If you and the other side are both agreed (probably in order to retain your own personal positions and not to lose face (if not faith) with those on whose behalf you act), then your formula will take the form of a non-communicative communique. Common examples (as useful in commerce as they are in government and in diplomacy), include:

> 'We have had frank and useful discussions' – which means that neither side said anything and that conversations were totally useless.

> 'Both sides explained their positions and the issues were most helpfully clarified'. Which means: neither side was prepared to budge; both wasted time in going over familiar and boring territory; and that the meeting was pointless.

> 'Representatives of . . . met at . . . on . . . The meeting lasted over . . . hours. Among matters discussed were . . . and . . . and. . . . Good progress was made. Both sides will be reporting back to their respective boards/companies . . . and it is anticipated that a further meeting will take place in due course. Both sides are satisfied with progress made in their full, frank and friendly consultations.' Which means: both sides could only agree that no one should be informed of anything which was not already public knowledge; that the meeting was uncommunicative and a waste of time and that any repetition should be delayed for the maximum possible time.

Finally: create diversions. Any parent will know that you do not simply say to a child, 'Stop doing that'. Instead, you try, 'It isn't really much fun smashing my mini computer. Look, have a go at this new toy I've brought you . . .' Or, 'Let me help you set up your monster museum.'

Grown ups (as an ex-Minister once exclaimed) 'are people who have advanced from infancy to adultery'. Treat them accordingly. Divert their minds and their attention. Do not say, 'No, I won't speak to you about this.' Instead, try, 'Let's discuss that'. Or, 'Let's have a go at the other.'

So recognize that while communication is a vital art, it is matched by that of non-communication. For success, you must practise both.

29

Never Walk Out

'Janner's Law on Dismissals' – 'Never Resign', at least unless you have a better job to go to. Anyone who resigns will normally lose all statutory dismissal rights.

The same rule generally applies to politics. On his hundredth birthday, I asked the redoubtable Lord (Manny) Shinwell, whether it was true that in 1948, when he was Minister of Defence, he had threatened to resign if British troops were not pulled out of Palestine. 'Certainly not,' he replied. 'I have neither resigned nor threatened to resign over anything. If you do that, my boy, you lose.'

In the art of communication, too, if you resign, pull out, walk out, break off relations – you normally lose.

There are, of course, exceptions to this as there are to all other good rules.

- If you are pushed out of your job and 'resign' because you have no alternative, then you are 'constructively dismissed' and will retain your dismissal rights.
- Anthony Eden resigned from a pre-war Cabinet because he backed Churchill's unrelenting, anti-Hitlerian stand. He returned later, eventually to become Prime Minister.
- If your communications deteriorate into deadlock, you may have to bring the other side to its senses by withdrawal from the negotiating process.

Still: In general, ideas can only go in and out of open minds and words of open mouths and ears.

For years, I have worked for the release in the Soviet Union of those Jewish people who wish to emigrate, in accordance with international law and even (in theory) the rules of the Soviet Union itself. I have never believed in the cutting off of communications with the USSR. We must retain communication or lose the chance to save lives. People go out through open doors, even though the Soviets continually refuse my wife and myself visas to enter through them.

As with laws and doors and politics, so with communications, public and private. It seldom pays to walk out.

For top people and businesses, TV is the essential medium for modern communication. With luck, skill, training and flair, you too could become a Reagan, if not a Wogan. Those who mess up their opportunities start at the top and finish finished.

The most celebrated and disastrous TV walkout was that of poor John Nott, then Defence Secretary in the days of the Falklands War. He upped and offed – and shortly thereafter, limped forever off the political stage.

Yasir Arafat was once interviewed for British television. Pressed too hard as to whether he would or would not recognize the right of the State of Israel to exist, and if so, then under what circumstances, he rose and departed. No viewer – and there were millions of them – felt that his flight enhanced his case. Apparent courage in the face of TV confrontation requires firm cultivation.

Still, it takes guts to walk out, especially when you are wired up for sound. For most of us, it is the mind, not the body, that departs. The fear of that moment dries the mouth and makes the tongue cleave to its roof.

Conversely, once you recognize that the ruder your interrogator may get, the more the viewer will incline in your sympathy, the greater your own security will come, and the saliva will flow again.

I have been taught by a remarkable tutor called John Goss, who for years trained British diplomats in TV techniques. A fellow member of the Magic Circle, he calmed my confrontation terrors by emphasizing the following theme:

When people watch TV, they do so in their own homes. So when you are questioned on the box, people instinctively feel as if you were sitting at home with them. That is why people say hello to live TV personalities as if they knew them. They are part of *their* lives.

Once you are in people's homes, you are their guest. They like their guest to be well treated; and if you are bullied or treated with rudeness, this they will resent.

If you are ill treated by an interrogator, fear not. No harm will come to you in the eyes of the viewer. On the contrary: provided that you keep calm and respond with courteous dignity, you will win.

Do not even contemplate walking out. Sit tight; keep cool; and fight back with sense and with sensitivity. You will be invited back into the studio; the interviewer has lost.

Apply the same rules to any other stage, in the communications world – from the across-the-table, eyeball-to-eyeball, to the major meeting. Lose your calm and you have lost all.

As a young soldier, in the British Army of the Rhine, I spent my Sunday mornings as a volunteer teacher in the school in the Bergen Belsen Displaced Persons Camp, a mile away from the awful concentration camp itself. The pupils came from a dozen countries and spoke as many languages. Their age range was as diverse as their opportunities for learning had been, during their years of miraculous survival; and they had no objection to tormenting their tutor.

One day, the English teacher, brought out to Germany by the Jewish Relief Unit, came into the mess, crying. 'Today, I really taught them a lesson,' she sobbed. 'I told them – if you don't behave, I shall leave. Their behaviour got worse, so I've left! That will teach them!' Which was not a point of view which was widely shared! The walk-out is usually as unsuccessful and as senseless as the drop out.

When a friend suggested that a certain wealthy man should 'stroll over and see him', the millionaire retorted, 'God would not have invented the automobile if he had intended me to walk.'

Oscar Wilde once explained that whenever he felt the inclination to take exercise, he would lie down until it passed off. If you feel the inclination to walk out, sit tight until it disappears.

30

Do Not Steal the Thunder

Every communication has its purpose. Stick to that purpose and do not trespass on other people's territory. Do your job and do not interfere with other people's right to do theirs. For instance:

- When introducing speakers, do not make their speeches. The Chair should control and run the meeting, but not take over the role of the speakers.
- If you call on the proposer of a vote of thanks, leave him or her to do the thanking. The following is as intolerable as it is sadly common: 'What a wonderful speech that was! Mr Brown, the applause that you have received is a clear indication of the appreciation which all of us have for that wonderful present-ation. We are all most grateful to you for sparing so much of your precious time. Many thanks. I shall now call on Mary Black to propose the vote of thanks.'
- If you are speaking or presenting as part of a team, you should agree in advance on the ground that each is to cover. The audience will resent repetition. Do not force your colleagues into repeating by using their material or covering their points. Do not commit this error through lack of preparation. Team work requires team practice and preparation. Those who sow in teams will reap in success.

How, then, do you avoid thunder stealing? Start with thought-fulness. Recognize the wrong you could do, prepare yourself to avoid it, and think on your feet at the time.

Secondly, instead of taking other people's ground, prepare it for them. For example:

- 'It is now my pleasure to call on Janet Hill. She is an expert on . . . and will talk to us about . . . This is a crucial area for us because . . .'
- 'So I have talked to you about . . . Roger Smith will now show you how you can put this information to use . . . benefit from

these tactics . . . win by following these rules . . .'

- 'To propose the vote of thanks tonight, we have one of our speaker's closest colleagues, William Green. In thanking our speaker, I hope he will also tell us how he would put the advice that we have received to work for us in our organization.'

31

The Art of Ending

At the start of your communication, you create your relationship with your audience. You establish rapport, create interest, say what you are going to say. Then you say it. At the end, you say what you have said.

A Soviet dissident was advised by a veteran friend as follows, 'Don't think. If you think, don't speak. If you think and speak, don't write. If you think and speak and write, don't sign. If you think and speak and write and sign, don't be surprised!'

Add your signature to an East European dissent, and anything could happen. Leave it off your own communication and nothing will happen. A letter requires a signature? So does a spoken communication. Everyone signs letters. Too many communicators simply collapse at the end of their effort, with a limp, 'thank you'. It is the audience who should be thanking the speaker, not the reverse.

So how do you bring your communication to an appropriate end? Easily: having started by saying what you are going to say; having continued by saying it; you end by saying what you have said. You summarize.

The summary is brief. It mounts up to its climax, like a symphony approaching the final clash of cymbals.

General de Gaulle once described life as 'a great voyage, which ends in shipwreck'. Too many fine presentations collapse at their conclusion, simply because the presenters do not trouble to compact their message and to leave their audience with minds alive.

When you prepare your communication, pay special attention to the beginning and to the end. If your thoughts are structured, the middle can take care of itself. Your message must be well thought out and rammed home.

The surest route to failure? Tacking on a series of ill-prepared, ill thought out conclusions. The after-thought is the death of a good ending.

'In conclusion,' says the speaker. The audience awaits the message.

'Which reminds me. . . .' Never admit that you needed a reminder, as the end of your communication approaches.

'Finally. . . .' But you have already said 'in conclusion', and that should have meant what it said.

'To end, then. . . .' But you already have done so, several times.

'Just one more word. . . .' Why say so? If you must add a word, do so.

Experienced listeners beware of the speaker who begins by saying, 'I shall not speak for long', or, 'Tonight, I shall be brief'. That is the normal prologue to a lengthy misery.

Equally, the speaker who finally and in conclusion, before coming to the end has a last word, reaches a series of false climaxes and endings, one after the appalling other, will crush the message under the weight of afterthought. Which is the precise problem. Had the thought been before and not after, the ending would have been climactic and not unworthy.

Listen to any fine speaker and you will find magic at the end. In Ecclesiastes, the Prophet says, 'Better is the end of a thing than the beginning thereof'. In a communication, however good the beginning, if the end is bad, the message dies.

Part III

COMMUNICATION AT WORK

32

Worker Involvement

Communication is involvement, not least in the workplace. Before turning to the sharing of information with employees, consider the background, as reflected by practice in other lands.

Discussions, consultations, meetings, communications – all these take time. At one end of the spectrum are those companies which devote no time at all to this process; at the other is Yugoslavia.

The process of worker involvement in Yugoslavia is massive and eternal. On the one hand, it is claimed that by the rule of the workers themselves, achieved through meetings galore, the work force not only has a real share in the success or failure of the enterprise, but the knowledge of that power provides its own job satisfaction. Both for its own sake and in its results (say its proponents), the system is worthwhile.

'Rubbish,' declare its opponents. So much time is spent in communicating that there is little left for work; little work done; and an economy in a mess.

The truth lies somewhere between the extremes. From the viewpoint of work satisfaction and worker involvement, it is not easy to have too much communication. But Yugoslav committees (many are prepared to admit, if only privately) push against the boundaries of human endurance. Communication is not always a pleasurable, amusing or gripping experience! Its success, when imposed through committees, is often inversely proportional to the frequency and length of the meetings.

Still, if you believe that democracy does not only mean the right to vote in local and national elections – that is, to a measure of control over your life when you are not at work – but also at least some right to decide how your working life is organized, then the Yugoslav system certainly achieves that result. People elected into and maintained in authority by their colleagues are extremely powerful.

Some years ago, my son and I spent a week studying worker participation in Yugoslavia. At its end, we took a cab to the airport of that fabulous walled city, Dubrovnik. En route, I put my report onto my trusty dictating machine.

On arrival at the airport, we were promptly arrested as spies. The cab driver, it transpired, believed that I had been transmitting messages on a portable radio!

I produced my credentials, as a Member of Parliament and a guest of their Government Ministers. The towering men who interviewed us showed no interest whatever. Then I produced the card, given to me by the manager of the hotel where we had stayed. I explained how he had shown us how the hotel was organized and run by his comrades and himself. Smiles broke out and we were let out.

A similar system, without the compulsion, rules the lives of Israel's kibbutzniks – the people who live on those communal farms which are the epitome of effective and accepted socialism in action. All decisions are taken either by the members or by those whom they elect. The larger the kibbutz, the more elaborate the communications structure.

The Federal Republic of Germany has another system of worker-involvement which has worked well for long enough to have become part of their remarkable post-war industrial revival. Our own Control Commission for Germany (CCG) was presented with a clean industrial slate. Determined to destroy for ever the power of the steel barons of the Ruhr, the CCG set up a system which could well have been used for our own industry, were it not for our own (happily very different) traditions. If you are studying potential systems for worker involvement in your business, we recommend a visit to the Federal Republic.

So with those few examples of sometimes extreme forms of worker communication, leading to involvement and a part in the decision-making process, now look at communication with employees in the UK.

33

Small Businesses

The definition of a 'small' business depends on the position from which you view it. Some legislation defines the term as businesses employing less than 10 people; some puts the line at 250. From the boardroom of a major company, any individual subsidiary with a turnover of less than a few millions is small; and indeed any contract, deal or problem which itself involves less than those same millions is unlikely to reach the group board. The success of the business will depend to a substantial extent on the nature and effect of communications between different levels within that organization. The type and the technique of those communications will differ with numbers, style and size.

In theory, the larger the organization, the more complex the communications. In practice, small organizations are often too overworked, too busy and sometimes even too politicized to communicate as they should. Recognizing that communicating within the small business creates in miniature many of the problems of the same process in a larger organization, consider some of the basic rules for the miniature enterprise.

First: lead. Your colleagues and employees will inevitably know if you are enthusiastically out front. There is no anonymity in a minnow pool. In a larger concern, you may remain in the shadows and leave others to do your communication. Not so when the business is small.

Whatever the size, leadership in any undertaking shines through. Captains of industry, like captains of ships, set the tone of their outfits.

'After me,' is the key call in any army; and the smaller the unit, the more directly it is heard.

Next: give individual attention to each person. The busier you are, the more your colleagues appreciate a moment of your time. The less you can spare it, the more effort you must give to its provision.

Try to treat your staff as if they were clients or customers. Avoid interruptions, wherever possible.

I find this much easier to preach than to practise. With my small group of lively colleagues, each ends the day with a pile of items to discuss with me. It requires a conscious effort to give time to each, without keeping others waiting for too long. Failure on my part invites frustration on theirs.

Which leads to: listening. Once again, treat the ear as the main organ of communication. In return, you will receive ideas, enthusiasm and loyalty.

Finally, remember that the communication among your colleagues themselves is continuous. They cannot escape from each other. The tinier the enterprise, the more claustrophobic it can become. You may not talk to them, but they will inevitably chat, discuss and gossip among themselves. Tune in.

Grievances grow great in small spaces. So cultivate comradeship, with your own time and concern. Then apply the same methods on a larger scale when your small business grows, as it deserves to do.

When my colleagues and I created our small operation – lecturing, writing, and publishing – we relied on frequent, casual contacts during the working day and some telephone calls at weekends. We quickly found that we were not communicating adequately. So we set up the following arrangements, which we recommend:

- A weekly 'diary session'. We bring together most of our staff. We start with any matters that we think should be discussed together; we then ask them for their contributions; then we open up the diary. Each item is checked, to ensure not only that all arrangements have been properly made and confirmed, but we also discuss, where appropriate, how each occasion should be handled. The process starts slowly, increasing its pace as the days go forward and the entries diminish. We try to look at least nine months ahead, together and weekly.

- The partners meet together once a week, quietly, alone and out of the office. Sometimes, we breakfast before a training session; sometimes, we lunch or dine; always, we spare time.

- The partners – and that includes myself – make a deliberate effort to listen to colleagues who wish to consult. That usually means getting out of communication with everyone else. No telephone calls and no interruptions, please.

This effort often fails. Emergencies must be attended to, and colleagues' crises are not always kept decently apart. Still, the effort ensures that complaints and frustration are less and efficiency and goodwill are greater.

All of which is fine, while the size of the business allows you to gather in groups or to consult individually. As it grows, so must procedures. Perhaps departments, divisions, units, shops or offices should have their own equivalent of diary sessions, on a frequent basis; executives might have to meet separately; while major gatherings are reserved for more infrequent or for special occasions.

Once there are more than about ten people in the business, its nature and atmosphere changes; it alters again at about 20; and so on, until one day your small operation – communicating sensibly within itself – expands and becomes a more major operation. This introduces different communication problems which we will tackle in succeeding chapters.

34

Listen to your Colleagues!

One of the great British myths is that employers' communication with unions is bad. On the contrary, with their employees' representatives, they usually speak often, informally and with reasonable frankness. It is their colleagues – executives and (especially) managers, at every level and particularly at the lowest – who too often are left groping in the business dark.

Not long ago, I addressed a meeting of the managing directors of a well-known multinational. Without exception, each was on first name terms with the convenor or other top union person in his outfit. Without exception, that person had immediate and almost unlimited access to him or at least to his office.

'Come in, Joe,' was the key phrase. 'Pleased to see you . . .'

Without exception, there was no such swift and relaxed access for any executive or manager, other than those at the very top. 'It wouldn't work, would it?' MDs protested. 'We'd never get anything done, would we?'

So executives rightly recognize that good industrial relations requires communication between management and unions or staff associations, at the top level. Wrongly, they leave their colleagues incommunicado.

Suppose, for instance, that rumours of redundancy creep across the shop floor. The convenor will head for the top boss and ask, 'Is it true?'

The MD may not come as clean as he or she could or should or even as the union would wish. But at least people and minds will meet.

Meanwhile, down on the farm . . . and back at the factory . . . here at the office – the same questions are asked. So why not get someone to see the MD?

Ridiculous. Queries must be directed to your immediate superior. If dissatisfied, then you can try the next level up.

Naturally, you will have to make an appointment. It wouldn't do for managers to wander in and out of executive offices, would it?

So what happens in practice? The manager consults the convenor. The convenor sees the boss and reports back to the manager and communication is achieved by a route both unintended and, to the manager at least, demeaning and totally unsatisfactory.

'That doesn't happen in my outfit,' you protest. Are you sure? Do you know? Would you know? How would you find out and who would tell you? And anyway, if doors are open to managers, then at what level do they close? It is the lowest levels of management that are the most disgruntled. Typical reasons why line managers, supervisors, charge hands and others are too often wretched are:

- They may earn less than at least some of the people they supervise. They have to work 'such hours as may be necessary for the proper performance of their duties', while their supervisees may get overtime, bonus, piece rates etc.
- They have little power – they cannot hire or fire and even their right to discipline is (inevitably and correctly) limited.
- Above all: who bothers to talk to them? Communication is fine, usually, at board room and at union level, but the lower the manager pecks, the less likely he or she will be to hear the cock crow.

A good communicator is a person who knows how to listen. 'He'll make time to listen to us, if he can,' goes the compliment. Conversely, the disaster, 'He never has time to listen to our problems.'

The moral is clear enough. Do not cut your communication cord at its lower levels. Stop, look and listen – then talk. If you are not able or willing yourself to be available to your colleagues, at every level, then make sure that someone else can do so in your place.

Secretaries and personal assistants are wonderful inventions, provided that they are not regarded as sound baffles, brickwalls or insulation, built around their bosses to keep them shielded from human contact. Employers by any name should not grow horns. They should develop antennae.

The story is told of a managing director who was afraid that he was going deaf. After a complete check up by an eminent consultant, the doctor took a carriage clock from the mantelpiece.

'Come over here, please. You hear this clock ticking?'

'Yes.'

The doctor walked back a few paces. 'And now?'

'Yes.'

The doctor moved to the door. 'Now?' he asked.

'Yes.'

Then the doctor moved out of the door and into the next room. 'How about now?' he called out.

After a moment, the executive said, 'Yes. But only just.'

The doctor returned to the room. 'Your hearing is fine,' he said. 'Your problem is that you don't listen!'

Listen and speak to your colleagues and the time used for both will be well spent.

Listening to your colleagues is more important than talking. A well known director was asked by a colleague how it was that he managed to see a great flow of visitors during his day and still get away from his office promptly at 5.30. 'I see fewer people,' he said, 'and I'm often stuck here until nine.'

'You talk back,' said the director.

Of course, response is a prime ingredient in the communication process. But as access to power is power itself, so the ear is a more important instrument than the tongue, in the practice of colleague communication.

35

Talking to Employees

Too many executives reserve too much of their communication with their employees for the giving of instructions or the imposing of discipline. If you want your staff, your workforce, your unions, your employees to feel and to work as part of the business, then keep in touch. How?

One to one, person to person, eyeball to eyeball, mind to mind – that, without doubt, is the most effective form of human communication. Unfortunately, though, it uses the most of that irreplaceable asset – time. So in practice and other than in the smallest of businesses, employers must communicate with their employees collectively.

One method is to share thoughts with the workers' representative – a convenor, shop steward, father of chapel, safety representative. The other: the group harangue, the meeting. To each and to both there is an art.

The approach is clear. Recognize that the union is the employee writ large. Your job is to look after the interests of the company, the board, the shareholders? Employees and their representatives must care for themselves?

A non-unionized individual is weak, even at your elevated level. Who would weep if you were sacked? Who would take industrial action, to seek your reinstatement? No one.

If you withdraw your labour, then the more choice your position, the longer the queue to fill the gap. Alone, the employee is lonely. Hence unions.

A union is a workers' organization. Its job is to protect workers' interests. At more refined levels they may call it a staff association.

When you communicate with the individual, non-unionized employee, you are in a position of power. You may exercise your might with benevolence or because you recognize that goodwill breeds good service. But subject only to those minimal rights to (for instance) unfair dismissal protection, you can act almost as you will.

Not so where the employee is represented by a union. Through unity comes strength. If one person withdraws his labour, so what? But a group withdrawal could be troublesome. The greater the disruption that could be caused, the more important it becomes to avoid trouble.

Communication is the best form of insurance against ill will and its results. The first rule: make it quick. If there exist swift, efficient and trusted ways for employees personally and collectively to ventilate their grievances, the greater the prospects will be of a sensible solution. Conversely, the worse the communication and the longer the time before the grievance is treated, the more likely battle becomes.

So establish your lines of communication and make sure that they are kept clear, by your colleagues and by you.

If workers can settle disputes without going to court, they will do so.

Next: when you deal with your workers, come clean. Recognizing that information and access mean power and strength, you start off with most of the trumps in your hand. But you only have to cheat once and you will forfeit the trust of those with whom you deal.

Do not underestimate the access which employees individually and unions collectively may have, to your information. If necessary, this may leak out through improper channels. It is likely then to be incomplete, incorrect and misinterpreted. So wherever possible, provide the facts, along with fair and honest explanations and interpretations.

Those who receive your communications may not like them. You may have to give bad news. But if you have the reputation for honesty, then at least you will win the basis of all acceptable communication – respect.

So communicate swiftly and with precision and truth. That leaves: tact.

As with all audiences, so especially with those over whose present and future you hold power, recognize their viewpoints, their interests and their rights.

I once listened with horror as a director informed his staff of the imminent arrival of computers. 'We are dragging the company, struggling, into the 20th century,' he announced, piling tired clichés, one on the other. 'We must modernize to survive. We can no longer use the inefficiency of human labour, where sophisticated machinery can do the job better and quicker.'

In each face I read the question, 'So who is to be sacked – me?'

The same talk to the same audience could have produced an entirely different and positive impact. 'Together we are going to look for ways to improve productivity, profits and pay. Together with you, the management is determined that the company will not merely survive but flourish into the computer age. In the long run, your jobs and ours depend on efficiency and that in its turn means bringing in the finest equipment.

'Far from seeking ways to reduce staffing, we are doing all we can to increase the strength of the company. People should not have to do jobs with which machines can cope better and more efficiently. We look to an increase in business to keep us all at work. But we need your help.'

So level with your employees and their representatives. Do not talk down to them. In your own way, you need them as much as they need you.

All skilled communicators know the importance of involving the interest of your audience. Methods include:

- As often as possible, use 'you' not 'I'; 'we' must mean 'you and us' and not the management, the board or company.
- Ask questions: 'What do you think? What problems are worrying you?'
- Seek advice and guidance, as you would from any other colleagues: 'What do you think? What would you do? How do you suggest that this could be better done, more efficiently handled, achieved in a more kindly or better way?'
- By all means tell them the risks and the problems if you must – but do not forget to mention the benefits, the advantages, the hopes as well as the fears.

In other and in briefer words, put yourself into the place of your audience. How would you react if someone with authority over you were to speak to you as you do to others? If the treatment would satisfy you, then and only then have you got the formula right.

36

Leading the Pack

From politics, the military through to business, leaders go out front and inspire others to follow behind. Their methods of communication are three: example, words – and successs.

Israel's small army has avoided destruction partly through the sophistication of its weaponry but mainly by the example and bravery of its young leaders. Their philosophy and reality is summed up in one word in Hebrew, two in translation *Aharai* – 'After me'. Leaders go first.

The alternative is disaster – when those behind cry 'Forward!' and those in front 'Retreat!' Gilbert and Sullivan's renowned Duke of Plazatoro led his disasters from the rear.

Leaders, then, communicate most and best by inspiring others to follow their lead. To copy is to flatter and we all copy those we admire.

Next: words. Bygone leaders addressed their tens or sometimes their thousands. Today's people of power talk to millions.

Moses, Christ or Mohammed, Socrates, Julius Caesar or Joan of Arc, Wellington or Napoleon; kings, queens or generals; priests or preachers – their words were limited by the power of their lungs or the pens of those who recorded their messages. Today, no leader of any stature can operate without the microphone and few without a radio or television. The voice and the personality of leadership is magnified, amplified, flashed by wire, through screen or satellite.

The most successful modern leaders know at least the basic techniques of presentational skills. They can think on their feet. They talk into microphones and before cameras, with skill and assurance.

Reading and leading are not the same. Only Churchill was able to proclaim speeches which read as well in print as they sounded by voice. President Reagan uses an invisible machine (an auto-cue) to carry his words before him, and as a trained actor, he reads as if his words were impromptu. But for most of us the read is dead.

Today's top leaders need training and skills in the professional techniques of public speaking, of radio and of TV. Consider the political collapse of Vice-President Walter Mondale, trodden into the electoral ground by President Reagan, on the broad screen. In politics, Mondale is a person of pose. Injected with the poison of the oblong screen, he stumbled and fell.

So it is not enough for leaders to be an example to others. They must project that example personally, on their feet and through the media. Their limits in leadership will be set by their failures on their feet, or before microphone or camera.

So the words from up front must be echoed back. And if the man, the mood and the moment coincide, success will follow. Followers and loyalty alike thrive on leaders' success.

Now apply these criteria to the leaders whom you have known, and assess their individual and relative stature against our three criteria. Churchill was out in the front lines, only restrained from the battle itself by those not prepared to risk his loss. His words were mighty and projected with unrivalled eloquence and style. His wartime success remains undimmed by his later electoral defeat.

Or take two captains of industry. One is a communicator who inspires his battalions, by example and success indeed but also through the enthusiasm, excitement and energy of his works and personality. The other is a shrewd accumulator of wealth, a master builder of commerce. But move him out into public life and he is clumsy. Unless he is too arrogant to recognize his own failures, he will also suffer the agonies of the dried mouth, the cloying tongue and the beaded brow when he is under the splotlight.

So successful leaders, out front, must also be skilled communicators. The public stammerer of tongue of stutterer of mind is unfit to lead.

The best quip about leaders? From that most outstanding of that ilk, Winston Churchill, in the House of Commons in September 1941. Commenting that leaders are often told that they should keep their ears to the ground, he growled: 'The British Nation will find it very hard to look up to the leaders who are detected in that somewhat ungainly posture!'

That said, leaders must listen. Otherwise they cannot marshal their followers into directions in which they already want – or can be induced to want – to go. As Henry Miller remarked, 'The real leader has no need to lead. He is content to point the way.'

When President Franklin D. Roosevelt died, Walter Lippmann wrote, 'The final test of a leader is that he leaves behind him in other men the conviction and the will to carry on. True leaders may be buried, but their communications live on in the mind and in the actions of others.'

37

Your Foot in the Door

Once you have your foot in the door, you can start selling. No foot, no sale. The communication equivalent is getting your audience to listen. Until they listen, they cannot hear. No hearing, no message.

So what are the techniques for forcing your audience to attend? How do you attract and keep the attention you need?

Remington boss and salesman supreme, Victor Kiam, tells the amazing story of how he, as a youngster, was one of some forty people invited to present products to an audience likely to be bored. So he brought a monkey; kept it hidden in a velvet cage; when he went into the room, he unveiled the monkey and let it loose among his audience, which collapsed into a mixture of laughter and panic.

Mr Kiam simply shouted out his message, 'Buy Pepsodent' or whatever, scooped up his monkey; and escaped before the arrival of either the police or the local asylum attendants.

I sometimes use magic as a somewhat more dignified variant on this theme, especially when talking to children. The scene: a primary school in Leicester. The time: morning assembly. The guest: the local Member of Parliament. All is silent as the head teacher introduces this boring emanation of Westminster. At which stage, I produce: magic.

Out come the disappearing bouncy balls, Leicestershire's woolly mouse, or even a prosaic ruler borrowed from a child and with sides apparently switching at will. The conjuring creates the rapport, and then the audience is prepared to attend.

Start, then, by interesting your audience, which means fixing your presentation on whatever interests them. Meeting an actual or potential client one to one? Then talk about his or her children. Addressing an audience? Do not begin until they are silent and watching you. Spare time for a word of greeting, an anecdote, a house-warmer. Then relate the subject directly to their interests. 'My theme is of direct concern to you, because . . . I shall suggest ways in which you can win more business . . . enhance your prospects . . . brighten your future. . . .'

From then on, watch your listeners. If their eyes wander from you and yours, drive them back. If you are the speaker, speak alone. Pause. Stop. Grab and hold the attention of your listeners. The best techniques include these:

- Change course. In that oil man's phrase, if you are not striking oil, stop boring. Tell them a joke, a story, an anecdote. Or
- Kick the ball into the crowd. 'What do you think, Mr Brown?' 'Have any of you suffered from this sort of irritation?' 'Miss Green, didn't you have to cope with a similar situation, last year?'
- If two people in your audience are talking, try walking up to them and simply smiling. 'Is there some point that you would like me to explain or to emphasize?' Two people are talking at the back. 'Can you hear me?' 'Yes, thank you,' the talkers reply. 'Fine,' you say. 'That's good. Because I can hear you too!' Better in most cases, though:
- Simply direct yourself, your attention or your words to the people whose attention has wavered. Ask them a question. The smaller the audience, the easier your task. But even with a large crowd, the technique is the same.

Not long ago, I addressed the European Tax Meeting of a leading firm of accountants, several hundred in a hotel ballroom. There were sporadic bursts of laughter from the back, obviously unrelated to my own multilingual wit. So I marched up the centre aisle; addressed myself to the miscreants, saying, 'And who are you?'

'I am Jean-Paul,' announced the main offender. Laughter. I had by happy chance lighted upon one of the characters of the conference.

'Please accompany me onto the platform, M. Jean-Paul,' I announced. They cheered the Frenchman as he followed me up the steps.

I seated him beside me and then put to him the questions which I was trying to answer.

A five minute double act ensured that the audience was and remained on my side and in attentive and happy silence. There were no more interruptions. I warned them that anyone who did so would be asked to change places with Jean-Paul.

This method has its obvious limitations. You must attack from a position of confidence and try to choose people who will not be offended. Watch your proposed victim with care and if he or she appears dignified or terrified, move on.

In a smaller audience, I prepare the ground by asking my hosts, 'Is there anyone here who is especially senior, or likely to be offended?' If so, then they get handled with care. By this route I also get told if a delegate is (for instance) hard of hearing or suffers from a stammer.

Conversely, I am often told, 'Don't forget to have a go at James Riley. He's a big chap who always sits at the back. He's got a marvellous sense of humour and will give you back far more than he gets.'

So play on your audience like the instrument they should be. Involve them. Vary your tone – monotone means monotony. Vary your pace and your content. Ring the changes and vary your act.

Which leaves props. In the communicator's vocabulary, that means visual aids. From the simple flip chart to the complex computer, from overhead projector to 35 mm slides, visual aids are not only useful to supplement sound with sight for the implanting of knowledge. They also tease and tweak the attention of your audience.

Beware, though, of the awful ease with which visual aids can take over a presentation and instead of bringing your audience into attention, simply allow it to sleep. Video films are the worst culprits, closely followed by slides. When the lights are off, eyelids droop.

As you build towards the end of your communication – the summary, the message, the climax – you must grip even harder at the attention of your audience. As at the start, so at the finish, watch their reactions and lift them up with all the enthusiasm, excitement and energy at your command. And as you pause before that last exhortation, that cadenza which will carry them with your argument – use every wile to grip their minds and their imagination. Call them with your eyes, your words, your message. Then, finishing on a high note, wait for the applause. You will have earned it.

38

References

The higher your perceived status and the greater the weight that others attribute to your views, the more sought-after you become for those who must offer references. So when and how should you best respond?

As a start, recognize that your obligation to provide a reference is entirely moral. Even former employers are not bound to say anything about former employees.

If you do respond to your moral obligation by providing a reference to someone who has a direct and proper interest in its contents, then the law effectively protects you from attack. If you speak ill of the person referred to, then that is defamatory. But as the statement is made on an occasion of 'qualified privilege' you have in reality little to fear. The person referred to will rarely be able to prove what you have written or said, there is no legal aid for defamation actions, and few of your victims could afford to seek justice out of their own resources. And as Oscar Wilde was only the most notorious to discover to his misery, defamation actions have a nasty way of failing.

In the absence of some unlawful motive – 'malice', as legally defined – the defence of 'qualified privilege' is watertight. If your statement was substantially true, you could in any event (but with some additional legal danger) plead 'justification'. And the combination of all these deterrents to action have meant that defamation proceedings arising out of employee references are almost unknown.

There is one main legal risk in reference giving. It applies largely to trade references or the like. You must avoid negligence or you could be successfully sued by recipients of your advice, who rely on it to their detriment, by the victim of your harmful and careless reference.

The public relations firm, Hedley Byrne and Partners, wished to invest a sizeable sum in a company, which referred them to its bankers, Heller & Partners. Heller & Partners said, in effect, that the investment was safe, but they added the usual disclaimer – that the advice was given 'without legal responsibility' on the part of the bank.

Shortly after, the company collapsed. Hedley Byrne maintained that the bankers owed them a duty to take care in the giving of the advice, even though it was supplied free of charge; that had they taken such care, the impecunious state of the company would have become obvious; that they did not take such steps and were therefore negligent and in breach of their duty of care; and that as a result, they had suffered loss, in the total sum invested.

Hellers vigorously denied negligence. In the alternative, they relied on their 'without legal liability' exclusion clause.

The Judge held that the reference giver does owe a duty to take care to see that the reference is accurate, even if it is supplied without charge. And (said the Court) Heller & Partners had indeed failed on this occasion to achieve that measure of care which could reasonably be expected of them. However, the exclusion clause bit. They were not liable.

So if you are ever in doubt about reference giving, follow the lead of banks, insurance companies, building societies and others who are frequent, unpaid purveyors of references. Put a note at the foot, 'While we are pleased to provide references for former employees (or as the case may be) all references are given without legal responsibility.'

So there is no need for you, your colleagues or staff to be anxious if you give a bad reference. Do not take refuge in the telephone, because calls are recorded and recordings are admissible evidence. Instead, use the disclaimer, and instruct your staff who give references to do the same and to expect disciplinary action if they do not.

Now suppose that you have decided to give a reference, for better or for worse. How can you best help the person who seeks it? Without question, by speaking personally to the would-be recipient.

The most respected method is the slightly apologetic and diffident. Thus:

'I hope you will not mind my writing/speaking to you about Mr Jones. I know that he is applying for a senior position with you. And I also know that you will have masses of applications. But it may possibly help if I tell you that I have known him for many years. If I had the sort of job to offer that he is applying for, he would certainly have it. And perhaps you might take this recommendation into account when you make your decision. Anyway, if you would like further information about Mr Jones, I shall be very pleased to provide it.'

What, then, of the people whom you only vaguely remember, but whom you would like to assist? As a Queen's Counsel and Member of Parliament, almost every former assistant and many acquaintances, however remote, think that it will help them to put my name on their application forms. Most of them are courteous and sensible enough to seek consent before they do so. I warn them that I can only tell the truth.

My integrity is their protection and can only be preserved by an honest response. So (I say) put me down if you wish. But if the recipients of the reference ask me what I know of your recent activities, I shall have to tell them. That reasonable and necessary approach disposes of many references. The rest take their chance.

If I am asked for a reference by someone whom I trust, like and want to help, but whose details I cannot remember, I often ask for a draft or a cv. 'Provide me with the information' I will say, 'and you can leave the praise to me!'

Commendations always come better from others. After a pæan of self-praise from his friend and composer, George Gershwin, pianist Oscar Levant quietly asked him, 'Tell me, George, if you had your time all over, would you fall in love with yourself again?'

Those who rely on references would do well to leave the affection and admiration to others, especially where a touch of perjury is useful. As Adlai Stephenson remarked, 'A lie is an abomination unto the Lord and an ever present help in trouble!'

If you bend the truth in your efforts to help others, then make sure that you are not caught. Or prepare to accept the consequences. Mitigate them with your disclaimers.

39

Communications Leaked

It is said that a government is the only vessel which leaks from the top. Not so. Boards of companies do too.

Leakages from any level occur when the vessel of trust is punctured, for one or more of these reasons.

- Carelessness. Example: you arrive for an appointment with a senior executive. He is delayed so his secretary ushers you into his office. She readily agrees to your using the telephone. You sit at his desk. It is covered with confidential documents. If your opponents at bridge do not hold up their hands but instead show you their cards, you turn away your eyes. Your host is showing his hand. Do you avert your eyes? Wartime Britain was plastered with posters reading, 'Carelessness Costs Lives'. In commerce, it costs confidences.
- Drink loosens tongues. In vino veritas. Beware of colleagues in their cups.
- Employees on the way out too often seek to pave their way to other jobs by explaining to interviewers what precisely they were doing in their present ones. This should be a major error. Those who do not honour the secrets of other employers are unlikely to do so with yours. So you would not employ them. Meanwhile, only saints are deaf to secrets.
- Worst of all, disgruntled employees, either on their way out or post-sacking, may joyfully take revenge by deliberately spilling every bean in the bag.

So industrial espionage is rarely the major source for commercial secrets. If you want to know what your opponents are up to, you could always ask them: they may tell you. When colleagues and I set up our own miniature publishing business, we were amazed and grateful for the readiness with which people in more or less the same line of trade were prepared to advise and to help us. I salute and thank them.

If you are not so fortunate in your competitors, actual or potential, then do not lower yourself into the world in which secrets are sold. Sit back and they will probably make their own way to you, unsolicited. Those who talk without due care or under the influence of drink, and those who seek jobs or revenge will probably produce all of the information you need.

40

Courts – Words with the Law

Whether you appear before the law as a witness or as an accused or as an advocate in an Industrial Tribunal or other arena where amateurs are permitted, the basic principles are the same. Clarity of speech and of thought and sincerity of manner are essential.

As a start, it helps to be heard. Speak up. Assume that someone on the Bench is hard of hearing and you will probably be right.

Answer the questions you are asked, where possible with a simple 'yes' or 'no.' Then elaborate. 'But I must add that . . .' or 'but please bear in mind that. . . .'

Do not try to be funny. Those who decide cases laugh last. But, of course, if *they* make jokes, it is usually wise to laugh.

Appearances always count. If you stand while giving evidence, stay still and do not slouch. If you testify seated, then sit up. And sit back, because that shows confidence, while sitting forward suggests apprehension or aggression.

Dress quietly. Reckon that those who sit in judgment are probably middle-brow and 'square' and you will not go far wrong. Dress as you would for the office and neither for the golf course nor for banquet, ball or disco.

If you present a case, whether as advocate or witness, be logical. Usually, it is best to tell your story in date order and events in the sequence in which they occurred.

Documents should always be in date order. Put yours into a bundle, clearly numbered, marked and firmly held together. You will need plenty of copies. If they are to go before the Court or Tribunal, then prepare one for each of the Bench; one for your opponents; at least one for your own side; and an extra, to pass to a witness. And do make sure that each document is legible.

Remember: contemporaneous documents are the best possible evidence of what happened at the time when they were made. All courts prefer to rely on documents, rather than on oral evidence. As a wise judge once put it, 'As time goes on, memory fades, but recollection improves!'

Obviously, the documents must be prepared well before your case is heard. Less apparently, so should you. Ask:

- Do you know your facts and your case? If not, learn them.
- Can you answer any question which you may be asked? If in doubt, get your lawyer or colleague, family or friend, to cross-examine you. Rehearsal and knowledge breed confidence, authority and success.
- Can you find your way around the documents, so that you can track down essential statements, without effort? If in doubt, keep reading through your bundle until you are totally familiar with it.
- Have you or your side assembled all likely witnesses and taken or obtained statements from them? If in doubt, ask your lawyer. In the long run, it is always better to prepare more statements and documents than you will need, rather than to discover your need too late.

Like a fisherman with his tackle in order, you are prepared to make the best of your expedition. If you are not used to the atmosphere of the court or tribunal, then try to visit it beforehand. Otherwise, arrive even earlier.

Try to sniff out the likes and dislikes of the particular person or people who will decide your case. Even a good lawyer cannot know all the law – that is impossible; good advocates and witnesses alike are those who know their judges.

So how do you find out? Try asking the usher or attendant. The more modest or apparently unimportant the person, the more likely it is that he or she will be flattered to be asked and will spare the time to answer.

Finally, do not allow your preparations for trial to include a communication with anyone who may sit in judgment upon you or yours. Remember the marvellous tale of the judge in a notoriously corrupt US city. At the start of a case, he rapped on his desk and made the following announcement, 'I have to inform you that I have received the sum of $10,000 from the plaintiffs and the further sum of $20,000 from the defendants. I must make it clear that I am not prepared to be influenced in my decision by money received. I am therefore returning $10,000 to the defendants!'

The parties had paid their premiums. The judge relied upon his own exclusion clause!

41

Telecommunication

How much could you improve your communication, within your organization and externally, by applying your mind and money to today's inventions?

In business, ignorance is never bliss. What you do not know, you do miss, and the adverse effect on your performance at work is incalculable. While the technologically unskilled find technical concepts and jargon formidable, most executives can, at least in principle, consider new options in telecommunications as they appear on the market.

So keep abreast of the field. Then bring in the experts to consult, install and instruct you and your staff to operate the equipment. Or: depending on your requirements, farm the work out. But do not evade the issue.

Traditionally, telecommunication meant telephone and radio, telex and television. The explosion of computer technology though, along with advances in audio-vision, have vastly widened the range of telecommunications options.

Start with your secretary. Your correspondence is word processed, and your organization's records are stored on disk. But is your computer linked to the phone?

The convergence of computers and telephones has revolutionized telecommunication. From the smallest office to the multinational participants in the 1987 Big Bang, communication has been streamlined by the integration of data and new ways of transferring information.

Example: with the help of a 'modem' attached to your computer, you – with your relatively inexpensive machinery – can have your secretary trace an obscure client on your data base at a moment's notice. The computer can dial their telephone number while your secretary gets on with other work.

Suppose a colleague urgently needs a copy of a contract. If you both have the right equipment, your operator can simply relay the information directly to your colleague's computer. Or: if the document happens to reside outside your computer's memory, it can be 'visually' phoned through – 'faxed' – to your colleagues's facsimile, assuming you both have access to one.

Whatever your occupation, to what extent will the instantaneous transmission of information, audio-visually or by text, internally or externally, improve your organization's performance? Have you put your computer and telecommunication system to full use, individually and together? What would it cost to upgrade and combine both systems to meet your telecommunication requirements?

In seeking out the most viable solution, think ahead. Choose the technology that offers the best opportunities for further expansion in your chosen area of telecommunication.

Do not buy anything that you will not use consistently. Telecommunication bureaux in all major centres cater for every need, from faxed and telexed messages to international conference calls. As technology develops, more companies use telecommunication, avoiding the time, cost and inconvenience of travel for short meetings. Why should executives and professionals meet physically, when they can see or speak to each other without moving?

I spend hours each day in my mobile office. Between my constituency, Parliament and lecturing, I work on the back seat of my car. For years, my dictating machine has kept me happily engaged, but I had to keep stopping to 'call in'. The car phone is a remarkable ally. When the power is on, I am in touch; when it is off, I can sleep.

Next: does your organization's success depend on quick access to research data, or to other forms of information? If so, then subscribe to an international library service, specializing in your field. You pay for time, and the information you need is communicated directly to your computer from the international data base.

Telecommunications companies offer a widening range of equipment and services. For instance: what kind of telephone or switchboard do you use? Or what of your office routine: can you cut down on the time spent answering or making calls? Should you install a new system, or improve your current one? Remember: obsolete routine means waste.

Then: telephone answering machines keep you permanently on

line – as do facsimiles. Wherever you are in the world, your bleeper can instruct your machine to play back messages and memos to you by phone. On business trips, telephone credit cards let you call clients, colleagues or your office, regardless of the currency or type of phone.

Telemarketing has become a catchword in sales circles. There is almost no limit to the kinds of products available by phone. Of course, most small companies have neither the space, staff, time or switchboard to accommodate extensive telephone sales. So, for either, or a combination of a flat rate or a percentage of sales revenue, telemarketing companies will prepare a script for you based on your corporate sales pitch, then sell your product. Without buying or hiring, and on condition that sales will justify the expense, your telecommunications network expands.

British Telecom offers more than 4,000 services and products to the consumer and business public. Yet the telecommunications revolution is only getting into gear. It spends hundreds of millions each year upgrading the public network, installing computer-controlled digital exchanges to replace the old switch units that connect calls through miles of underground cables. Soon, the full integration of computer technology into the public network will ensure that all customers will benefit from the full range of new hi-tech options.

At the very least, your phone will provide you with a more pleasurable audio experience. You will hear no interference, and your calls will be connected in a fraction of the time that it now takes. Your computers will access information at multiples of the speed that you now pay for – so phone bills should drop considerably. A fax that now takes half a minute to send will soon take five or six seconds, and the reproduction will be as accurate as a good photocopy.

The new digital system provides an important benefit for direct-line phones. The new 'Star Service' enables you to re-route calls automatically to another number, or to bring a third party on line at any time. You are alerted that another caller is waiting to get through, and finally, you have the option of choosing which call is most important, and putting the rest on hold. All on one line.

My advice: plan ahead. Human communication and tele-communications technology advance together.

Part IV

AUDIENCES

42

Choosing Your Audience

Preparation for communication means asking a series of questions:
What? When? Where? How? By whom? And above all, to whom?
Whose are the right ears in which to plant your message?

The famous black writer, James Baldwin, said, 'Consider the
history of labour in the USA – a country in which, spiritually
speaking, there are no workers, only candidates for the hand of the
boss's daughter.' Never mind her hand. If you can attract her ear,
you may achieve your end through one conversation.

Remember your Bible. When that wicked chief minister,
Haman, had determined to wipe out the local Jewish population, it
took the pleadings of Queen Esther to soften the heart of the King
and to turn the tables on the tyrant. Haman was duly hanged and the
King cast his cloak of protection over his Jewish community. It was
only the King who could make and who made the ultimate decision
of life or of death for his people.

When you have a communication problem, you must work out
who will decide on the fate of your proposal, project or scheme.
Who can make industrial peace or wage commercial war?

As in war, so in politics, personal or private, public or professional, business or commercial. Pinpoint your allies and your
adversaries. Either way, identify your target, then aim, steadily and
well.

Suppose that you need better relations with your company's
union. You decide that communication is essential, to get across
your point of view, the company's concerns, your view of the future
and your perspective. You may have a number of potential
audiences:

- The convener or other union chief
- The shop steward or Father of the Chapel or other union head of
  the individual unit.

- The area secretary or other full time and outside official who might be (from your point of view) more 'reasonable' than those who are closer to the battle.
- Your work force or some appropriate part of it.

Or suppose you need to carry your point of view at board meeting. You may neither have the time nor may it be politic to speak to all of your colleagues. So consider: who has the influence? Whose views will be respected? And who is articulate in their expression? Then, which of these important colleagues is most likely to be on your side on this issue?

'There are two things to aim at in life,' said a philosopher. 'The first is to get what you want; and after that, to enjoy it. Only the wisest of mankind achieve the second.'

You must communicate with the person whom you wish to influence. To enjoy the fruits of that influence, that is the supreme art.

43

Foreign Audiences

A Norwegian Prime Minister once affectionately proclaimed, 'We do not regard Englishmen as foreigners. We look on them only as rather mad Norwegians!'

Writer Quentin Crisp took a less charitable view of the non-British, 'I don't hold with abroad,' he said. 'I think that foreigners speak English when our backs are turned!' Anyway, if you travel abroad or greet foreigners at home – and especially if you wish successfully to export or to import – then talk you must.

To avoid the miseries of the Tower of Babel, you must start by choosing your tongue. In ordinary conversation, it matters not who makes mistakes or how. Precision comes second to goodwill. Do not be afraid to mangle someone else's language, rather than to talk your own. Your effort will be appreciated.

To find out how well you are doing in the foreign tongue, try speaking to strangers. When they reply in your own language, you will know that you have not only failed dismally to speak theirs, but your accent has even given away your own. Never mind, Bash on. The only way to learn to speak – in public or in a foreign language –is to practise. Inflict yourself on others and if you know the basic techniques, improvement should be yours.

The best way to learn? From children. They speak only their own language, and that in simple and essential words. I have learned several languages that way and still speak them all in the words of a child. Business and political talk then switches to English.

It is anyway better to discuss crucial detail in a tongue which to you is precise. Far too many international misunderstandings are based entirely on the interpretation or misinterpretation of words.

If you converse with or address foreigners in your own language, then at least begin and end with words in theirs.

I am Member of Pariament for part of the City of Leicester, about one fifth of whom originate from India, most from the state of

Gujerat. My speeches to their meetings and gatherings begin with: 'Bayo, baheno', (however spelled, it matters not). To the greeting of 'Brothers, sisters', there is always affectionate applause.

For the ending, what could be better than: 'Jai Gujerat, Jai Hind' Three cheers for the Gujerat and for India.

The Speaker of the House of Commons produced the equivalent climax, in his salute to King Juan Carlos of Spain, addressing both Houses of our Parliament. 'Viva el Rey! Viva Espāna!' Spanish or English, the audience responded with 'Viva!' – a tribute to the King, to Spain and to Mr Speaker.

If you do not know the essential words of greeting and of sign-off in the language concerned, ask someone trustworthy. Write the words carefully, sound by sound. Make sure, though, that your helper is not guiding you to inviting the audience to 'shove off', or worse!

Next: speak slowly. Whether you are communicating to foreigners in their language, probably if only occasionally mis-pronounced, or in your own, to which they must attune their unaccustomed ears, speak with precision.

For the skilled orator, the pause is an essential weapon. Never is it needed more than in battle with those who have the misfortune not to have been brought up in your native tongue.

Watch out especially for idioms or dialect, for terms which may be universally known in your country, but a mystery to your audience.

Humour, too, is hard in another language because so much is based on what the French call 'jeux de mots' – word play, or puns.

The ultimate rule, though, is to make fun of yourself and not of other nations, races or creeds.

I once began an after-dinner speech in Strasbourg, pronounced in my lamentable French, with the following, 'Madame Pflimlin asked me where I was born. I replied, "Pardonnez-moi, excusez-moi. Je suis anglais, mais ce n'est pas ma faute!" ' The audience forgave me not only for my English ancestry, but also for my terrible French. Since then, I have used the same story, duly adapted, in many tongues.

Finally, in your language or in that of your audience, keep your words brief, brisk and simple. 'Do as you would be done by'. Extend to others that courtesy in speech which you would wish from them.

44

Bank Managers

The essence of a bank manager's job is to lend the bank's money at an appropriate rate of interest and with minimal risk. Your dealings have two objects. First, to obtain the financing you need for as long as you need it; and second, to do so at the minimum cost. To each there is an art. Communication and cunning are the two essentials.

The best way to get money from bank managers is to convince them that you do not need it. The greater your perceived need, the tighter the manager's lips and the bank's purse strings.

So walk upright into your manager's office. You should never communicate with a banker from a kneeling position. Rise and show confidence. How? By precisely the same methods that you should use when dealing with any other audience. Cover your nervousness by direct eye contact, a firm handshake and a ready, opening smile. Recognizing that most bank managers are human, refer to their interests before you come to your own. 'How's the family?' 'You're looking very fit. Just back from holiday?' 'Did you hear the thunderstorm last night?'

If you have unwisely left getting to know your manager until your time of need, you will have to stick to generalities. If you had the foresight to lunch with him or her when times were good, then start with the more personal: 'I hope that Mary has completely recovered from her operation.'

As in a public performance, so in this private one. A little humanity at the start is a wise investment.

Then tell the manager what you want. As in most negotiations, start high. Even if you get the lot, you do not have to use it.

It will then be the manager's job to probe any project or purpose for which you need the finance. What is the risk for the lender? And then, what security can the bank obtain, to ensure the return of its money?

The more secure you appear, the less security you will need. The fact that you are asked does not mean that you need necessarily provide. As a young barrister, badly in need of money, I had to mortgage my little all to obtain a miniscule overdraft. The deeds of my already mortgaged home were lodged with the bank, to make sure that I could not obtain a second mortgage or other finance on the strength of the equity which remained. My inadequate life insurance policy was duly pounced upon. And even then, some kindly relative was invited to guarantee at least part of the loan.

Today, as a Queen's Counsel who would lose his warrant if he went bust, and who has operated a well regulated account for many years, all that is required is a telephone call.

Note, though, that 'well regulated account'. The banker will lend to those who operate their debts in a businesslike way. If you intend to draw beyond the limit or not to repay on a due date, tell the manager. Explain the circumstances. Make an appropriate request for extension of facilities or time or a promise to repay on an acceptable basis. Do not simply overdraw or delay repayment without warning. That is the banker's red flag of danger.

Conversely, if you can be trusted to handle your own money properly, and to give adequate communication of any potential problems, then there is good ground for lending you some of the bank's money.

'When I consider life,' wrote poet John Dryden, ' 'tis all a cheat; yet, full'd with hope, men favour the deceit; trust on, and think tomorrow will repay. Tomorrow's falser than the former day.'

Bank managers look at the former day. They trust on, only if yesterday gave grounds to hope that tomorrow you will repay.

Happily, bank managers and their bosses are usually kinder to their clients than many of us miscreants deserve. Compassion is rarely the reason. They make their living through accumulating interest on the money they lend, not from suing clients or disposing of their assets.

So even in adversity, you may not do badly from your banker. Advance upon him or her, head held high, confidence blazing from your eyes. Communicate your problem with that radiant frankness that got you your loan in the first place. The rescheduling of debts is a process happily not confined to nations. Good luck, then.

45

In the Chair

Communicating from the chair is a privilege, to be treated with skilled care. The essence of the art is to convey your wishes, to win your point and to impose your message, in a way that the audience –your colleagues, listeners, victims, allies or enemies – believe to be their own idea and in their own interests. You will need concentration and control.

Decide in advance – what do you wish to achieve and who will help you get it? What should be on the agenda and what left off and in what order should items be taken? Have you primed your allies and counted your resolutions? Do you understand and can you administer the rules of the organization, assembly or meeting? Have you arranged the best venue for your purpose and the most sensible seating for your audience? Have you an intelligent ally at your side?

If your preparation is complete and you know the subject, the venue and the audience, you can then concentrate on the meeting, the audience, the subject being discussed. Never allow your attention to waver or you are done. Preparation and concentration lead to control. This in its turn requires apparent fairness, the balancing of debate, the giving of a hearing to minority opinions and to those who express them and the assurance for each participant that his or her presence is essential and appreciated.

The audience expects you to ration time so that the business is well done and within the hours available. They start on your side. Keep them there.

Company meetings invariably operate by concensus; trade union and most political gatherings, by vote. If you are in the chair at either and fear losing, there are other questions to ask:

Should you adjourn the discussion and hope that a different result will be achieved when heads have cooled and you will have time for some more lobbying? Should you refer the problem to a committee, a commission or to a wise individual for consideration? Should you lay your prestige on the line and hint at or actually threaten resignation if you lose?

Rubber stamp meetings are boring. Participants leave disgruntled, often never to return. Dictatorship is a convenient form of government for a country or a corporation and may be more efficient. But it is also unpleasant, unhappy and usually highly resented and eventually doomed.

So control your meeting, resolve the differences, seek concensus, sense the feel of the meeting and always try to let the participants believe that they have a valuable part in it.

Communication through listening is not easy. But nowhere is it more important than from the Chair.

46

Getting the Best from your MP

To get the best from MPs requires a combination of knowledge, persistence, cunning – and skilled communication. As their services are free and far more valuable than generally appreciated, presentations to your parliamentarians are well worth some careful study.

Only your own Member can officially intervene on your behalf. By firm and intelligent convention, they each look after their own constituents and requests for help from other people's get passed on.

Your MP is either the one who represents the area in which you live or the one who represents the area in which you have your business. In the first case he or she is concerned because you are a resident voter and in the second because you provide employment for constituents.

As most MPs are human, they react well to self-interest – they wish to keep their jobs. So you could start your letter, 'I have always voted for you, but . . .', or 'I am sure that you would not wish to lose the support of my family/community/Chamber of Commerce . . .', 'We employ a large number of your constituents, but their jobs are at risk . . .', and so on.

Do *not* offer any material inducement of any sort whatever. You cannot buy off trouble – and any attempt to buy favour from an MP is likely to rebound swiftly and permanently. Even modest gifts – like the famous silver teapot, reputedly once discovered in the airing cupboard of Labour Minister Tony Crosland – may cause embarrassment.

So you decide to approach your MP: perhaps for help in getting or keeping government contracts, or to apply proper pressure on the local authority in a planning matter. Whatever your problem, the cost of your MP failing to solve it could not be more than a couple of stamps and as much of your own time as you wish to devote to his cultivation.

How then do you best approach your MP? First line of attack: write to your MP at the House of Commons, London, SW1. Keep the letter short. Most MPs have minimal time and less assistance. Keep the details to an attached schedule or brief – which should be just that: brief.

See your MP at a surgery or advice bureau. Details are usually available from his local party office or from his agent. You will then join a queue, unless you can arrange to see him either shortly before or after the general mêlée.

Regard this meeting as an ice breaker. The bigger the queue, the less time there will be for you. Introduce yourself and your problem, bring details in writing and suggest that you fix a further appointment at the MP's convenience, in the constituency or at Westminster. 'I know how busy you are this morning – the managing director and I will be delighted to call on you, whenever you may wish. . . .'

Call on your MP at Westminster. If you have not fixed the appointment in writing, then confirm it by letter.

Telephone the House of Commons – 01 219 3000. Ask for Members' Message Board. Leave word for the MP to phone you back. MPs have free telephoning facilities for constituency purposes. A cunning but disliked method of getting a reply from the reluctant is simply to leave your name and telephone number with the message 'urgent constituency matter'. Curiosity should procure you a response.

What can the MP actually do to help? Here are some possibilities:

- A letter from an MP to central or local government, or to a company will set alarm bells ringing. It will carry your complaint to the top. A Minister, for instance, will answer an MP; he will sign the letter and be responsible for its contents.
- Your MP may 'raise the matter in the House'. This may be done in one of four ways. First, he or she may put down one or more parliamentary questions, either for written or for oral answer. Secondly, your MP may apply for an adjournment debate – an end-of-the-day half hour devoted to constituency and other problems, and balloted for by back benchers. Or he or she may set down an Early Day Motion – to be debated on a day which is never reached, but which will achieve publicity for the cause. Finally, your case can be used as the basis for a speech in a debate, or a private member's bill, or in a '10 minute rule bill',

which (once again) cannot become law but makes much potential noise in the course of its promotion and collapse.

● Your MP may launch straight into a campaign through the parliamentary press corps. If access to the media represents power, then MPs – especially locally but also nationally – enjoy *both* that power and its use.

The MP will decide – either alone or in conjunction with you – whether and if so how to present your case and whether inside the House or outside it. But your communication to MPs should be designed to awaken, attract and maintain their interest; to provide them with minimum information with maximum impact. Then supply further, updated material, as and when they require it.

Please do remember that most MPs are overworked and under-staffed, anxious and willing to help but deluged with demands upon their time, and that Members' best weapons are their wastepaper basket. To keep your communications out of the bin, keep them short and to the important points.

47

Civil Servants and other Experts

If you need information or help from a Government Department or from a local authority, you must know the following:

- What questions to ask?
- Where to find the answers?
- Who can help you?

As a young barrister, I was interviewed by my future head of Chambers, a wily and experienced old lawyer.

'Do you know your law, my boy?' he demanded.

'Well, I hope so,' I replied, innocently. 'I have a law degree. I managed to pass my Bar finals. I spent a year studying law at Harvard.'

'Your answer shows that you know nothing!' he retorted. 'Every barrister should know that he does not know the law.' He pointed at the serried ranks of law books, lining his walls. 'Look. Dozens of volumes of Statutes. Hundreds of volumes of case law. Textbooks. Precedent books. Rule books. No one can possibly know the law.

'No. A good barrister is not someone who knows the law. He or she is someone who knows what law to look for; and where to look for it. And who knows the Judges!'

As with the law, so especially with the civil service. You cannot know (for instance) even the basic entitlements of citizens from the Department of Social Security. You can know how to find out what rights are availabe, from where and from whom. You should also know the route to the right person, if your efforts may or do go wrong.

Your communications with officials should first recognize that all of them have a due and proper regard for the importance of their own departments, units and functions. So treat them with respect. Talk up, not down.

A civil servant should be both civil and a servant. But civility and servility are miles apart; and service varies, along with the individual who is to provide it or to supervise its provision, and the way that he or she is approached.

For instance, suppose that you have a complaint about the way that you are treated by some junior clerk. You know the local head of the department? You could have a quiet word, but if the official ever finds out that you communicated at the top without giving the lower levels the chance to put their mistake into order, you will acquire a new enemy. Enemies, like friends, should be chosen with care and not acquired through negligence or lack of tact.

So go first to the individual, if possible. If that fails, try that person's superior. Then (and only then) go to the very top.

As a new MP, I received a complaint about a constituent's treatment at a local hospital. I wrote a letter to the appropriate Minister. He contacted the hospital; obtained an explanation; and sent it through to me.

When I next visited the hospital, the Head Administrator took me quietly on one side. 'I'm sorry that you wrote to the Minister about the case of . . .' he said. 'Of course you were fully entitled to do so. But I would so greatly have appreciated the chance to put matters right, without getting into trouble at such a high level!' He was right. I was wrong. I learned that you must select your level of communication, with care and with understanding for the failings of others.

That said, top access is essential. You may have this individually or through the head of your company or organization. Or you may achieve it through your Member of Parliament.

I once asked the Manager of the local DHSS office what happened when a letter came in from an MP. 'The alarm bells ring,' he answered. 'I deal with the case myself.'

Access is power – for evil or (hopefully) for good. You may have it yourself, through your contacts, your friendships, your relatives. Use it for others, with good sense. Be doubly careful when you use it for yourself.

The power to communicate at top level, individually or through an MP, is a crucial democratic right. It is at its best when the constituency system operates as it should. To abuse that system for personal gain, however, is wrong, and sometimes it is also a criminal offence. Remember, corruption is not confined to the giving or receiving, attempting to give or to obtain, money or a benefit in kind. Any sort of 'favour' is enough.

So when you communicate privately, ask yourself what would happen if that communication went public. The moment you communicate a secret, you risk exposure.

Remember, then, that civil servants and others in public life – whether voluntary and elected or professional and appointed – are especially vulnerable. Recognize their sensitivities; know what to ask them, when and how; and you deserve good results.

Now for the response of civil servants themselves. I asked a number of them, 'How should people communicate with you, so as to get the best results?' Happily, they agreed with my above suggestions, but here are some additions, from them.

First: make full disclosure. That means: explain precisely what you want and why you want it. Come clean. The more information you provide, the more likely you are to get the additional information – or the advice – you need.

It also means declaring your interest, if you have one. It is no crime to make a living, to expect some personal gain from the approach you are making. It is wrong not to reveal that fact.

If, for instance, you have a professional interest in the case, say so. 'I am his lawyer . . .' 'I represent her accountants . . .' 'This planning problem affects me . . . my home . . . property that I own . . .' 'I am a director/shareholder in that company . . .'

Members of Parliament and local councillors are required, whether by tradition or by law, to declare an interest in subjects about which they speak or make representations. Others should do the same.

Second, seek out the responsible person – that is, the individual who can make the decision which concerns you or your case. The time to go to the top is if you have got nowhere lower down.

If you do not know whether you are going to the right person, say so. 'If I have gone to the wrong department, my apologies. I would be grateful if you would pass this enquiry onto the appropriate person.' Or telephone, 'Who is the right person to speak to about. . . ?'

If you know that what you are asking about affects different authorities, write separate letters. Cross reference between them, if you wish. Even send copies of each of the letters to the others. They may have to liaise among themselves, but if there are separate questions, which should be addressed to separate departments, put them into separate letters.

For example, people often write one letter about National Health Service problems, National Insurance contributions, pensions and other benefits. Each should have a different destination. Communicate with the correct people, for each enquiry or complaint.

So take steps to try to ensure you have the right person. If you are not sure, say so. Give an indication and the recipient will take the necessary steps. Do not begrudge separate letters to different people or departments, on different queries.

Third, whoever you may be writing to, keep your language simple. Officialese is going out of fashion among officials; it is far too common among citizens who write to officials. For some reason, people believe that you have to be pompous, if you are dealing with officials. Not so.

Avoid, for instance, the following:

- Pursuant to my enquiry of the 8th instant . . .
- With reference to your letter of the 18th March and with particular reference to paragraph 8 thereof . . .

And all other long-winded or hackneyed terms of expression.

If your letter or approach is sensitive – whether as to price or otherwise – say so, with complete clarity. If it is not, avoid putting 'Private and Confidential' onto envelope or letter. Leaks are possible, but in general you can trust that matters which you clearly indicate are sensitive will not go further.

Finally, always provide a contact point. Specify a telephone number so that the official or his or her representative can get in touch with you speedily without protracted correspondence.

Communication in both directions requires sensitivity and common sense. It is well worth the care, thought and effort.

Part V

PUBLIC COMMUNICATION
AND THE MEDIA

48

Radio and TV

Communication on radio and television is a skilled craft, to be approached with care and with training. How, then can you make the best of your chances on the air?

Where possible, choose your programme. Know your market and how you are most likely to reach it – and know your interviewers and who is most likely to be helpful.

The worst interviewees in any category are those who do not know their subject. Most occasional or amateur broadcasters are interviewed and all interviewers operate on the adversarial principle. Whether they are the devil's or angel's advocate depends upon the person, the subject and the occasion. Their job is to probe and to seek out facts and opinions. If you do not know your facts, you will get no respect for your opinions.

Strangely, business people often get bottom marks for knowledge. They may be expert within the narrow and limited confines of the subject about which they want to talk. But interviewers place themselves in the listener's place and look on the broader scene. So if you do not want to get floored by an unexpected question, do your homework.

Time on the air is an extremely expensive commodity. You will be offered yours free of charge, so do not abuse the hospitality. You will only come late once for a programme, a producer or a station. You will not be asked again, nor will they be the least interested in even the best of excuses.

The importance of being early is not merely to avoid coming late. It also enables you to settle in, to reduce panic, to chat up the staff and (if possible) your interviewer – and especially to discover the intended main lines of your unscripted contribution.

Hopefully, your interviewers will be on time. If the programme is going out live, then to be late may cost them their jobs. But their schedules can go amiss in the same way as yours. The only difference is that you are in their kingdom and they are entitled to be late – you are not.

The ultimate in reporter lateness provided me with one of my few and cherished (but as yet unrealized) chances to enter the *Guinness Book of Records*. Some years ago, I arrived my customary few minutes early for a local radio recording session. The engineer was there but the reporter was not. Half an hour later, he had still not appeared. I then made my revolutionary suggestion to the man in charge. 'Let me interview myself!' I asked. 'I promise to ask myself the nastiest and most probing questions. And you can dub in the reporter's voice when he turns up!'

To my delight, he agreed. I carried out the interview with immaculate courtesy, but dug away at my own weak points, being sure, of course to provide succinct and appropriate answers. When the interviewer turned up, he used judiciously the miracle of the razor blade in the cutting room. His questions were duly dubbed into place.

Ask how long your contribution will last. Do not despise the sixty second plug. Just as one photograph in a newspaper is more effective than ten columns of print, so a minute on the air is worth reams of advertising copy.

The briefer the appearance, the more concisely you must make your points. So work out in advance those points that you are determined to make. Slot them into as few sentences as possible. Then be prepared to expand on each, if you are given the chance. Make notes by all means – but unless you are reading a pre-prepared and timed contribution, you do not prepare a word-for-word script. Not only will it sound contrived if you are given the chance to read it, but you will probably have to work without it. And if you are used to leaning on your crutch you will miss it when the interviewer forces you to cast it aside.

If you are asked to give a scripted talk, then it will probably have to be timed, if not to the second, then to the thirty seconds. It will require the producer's approval.

So have your script typed in double spacing on A4 paper or its equivalent, with plenty of copies. Stick to the theme that you have been given and keep your commercials reasonably subtle. Think about your audience and what the producer wants you to put across to them.

When you have prepared your piece, read it out aloud; time it on a stopwatch. Remember that you are better off to put less across well than to pack too much into too short a broadcast.

Read your script over to a tape recorder and play it back. Get your wife, your husband, your children or your close friends to criticize.

If you use a script of notes in the studio, you must carefully avoid paper rattle. Do not turn pages. Lift each sheet gently from the pile and place it noiselessly to one side.

When reading your script you must project your eyes and your mind ahead. So make sure that you do not allow a sentence to run over from one page to the next. End a paragraph and a page together.

Be prepared to amend your script even at the last minute, so as to make it topical. For instance, I broadcasted four early-morning three-minute religious items – affectionately known as 'God spots'. Each day, the producer asked me to lead in from current news – terrorist bombs, religious festivals, anti-nuclear demonstrations or whatever was in the headlines. And the programme presenters added their comment at the end, so that each presentation finished with a chat. Even when you are carefully scripted, you should prepare for flexibility.

Most of the rules and advice already given in the context of radio apply equally to TV. But we now add to sound the dimension of sight. Presentational stakes pile high.

Every peril in radio presentation is concentrated, condensed and made (literally) visible by the oblong screen. Almost every rule that we have so far considered for sound applies equally when it is accompanied by vision.

TV studios vary from the small and comparatively cosy to the vast stage. You may be shown into a modest room, ushered to a chair and filmed by a single camera. Or you may discover yourself literally on stage, with a captive studio audience – or, more likely, in a hangar-like hall, bestrewn with cables and wires and over-populated with wheeled cameras and hyperactive people, many of them dressed like men from Mars, earphones attached to their heads, wires to their bodies and clipboards to their hands.

Be not afraid. They are probably more terrified than you. Not only do their jobs and reputations depend upon their success but they know all the traps. Just as the best hypochondriacs are doctors, so the most terrified TV performers are professionals.

Special tip: When you see the signal of 10 seconds to go, take a deep breath; let it out slowly; and you will find that you are relaxed when your turn comes.

To prepare for a specific programme, you need to know where and when it is being held; its shape and your part in it; who will do the interviewing and in what format – for instance, individual, panel and/or confrontation?

So telephone and ask and write down the details in case you forget. If in doubt, say: 'It looks fine, but I'll double check with my diary and phone you back within the next ten minutes.' Get the person's name and number and think, fast.

Will the programme help you, your company or your case? If it will mean cancelling some other work or activity, would that be worthwhile? Should you step back and recommend someone else in your place? If you cannot get to the studio, can you induce them to come to you or, more probably, let you go to a more convenient place?

Would you prefer the interview to go out live or would it be better pre-recorded? If you go ahead, will you really have the chance to put your case . . . to make your presentation fairly . . . to explain your problems . . . to get some free advertising . . . to build your reputation or perhaps even to earn a fee? Or are you simply letting yourself in for an unwanted brow-beating, perhaps on a subject about which it is better to keep a low individual or corporate profile?

If in doubt, take a chance. Do not 'decline' or be 'unavailable', unless you really have no comment to make or you cannot be available, in which case, explain your reasons frankly.

The best way to learn television techniques? Make your communication in front of a video camera and play back the result. Criticize it yourself and then get an expert to explain how to put the matter right.

Next best: just switch on the television and watch other amateurs performing. Switch on your own critical faculties along with the set; take pen in hand; and jot down the notes. Here is a list culled from a normal quarter of an hour of watching news interviews:

- Do not smirk when introduced
- Do not move from the centre screen
- Do not fidget
- Do not lose your concentration, even for a moment.
- Do not look at the screen – eye your interviewer – ask for an eye line.

Arrive on time and properly dressed.

Prepare yourself and your case. Best of all: train for the task, learn how to do it, from experts. Then hope for the best.

49

The Press

How could and should you handle your communication in the press, making the best of newspaper people and the world of print?

Essentially by doing unto them as you would have them do unto you. With rare exceptions, reporters and editors will react to kindness with generosity, to hostility with patience, to trust with respect, to confidence with confidentiality, but to contempt and ridicule with either silence or unfavourable coverage.

Newspapers live by finding and printing news. Churn out for them the old, worn, cliché-ridden press releases and they will be 'spiked', filed, binned, left unused and useless.

Produce a story that is new . . . news . . . alive . . . and aimed at its market . . . and it has at least a reasonable chance of life.

To sell products, you study markets. Apply the same principle to your presentations for the media. Who are the people whom you really want to reach? Which newspapers are most likely to take what story? Which editor or reporter has a personal interest in a particular theme or idea?

By all means get to know the newspaper people – editors, news editors, feature editors, reporters, full-time or freelance. Ask for their help and you may well get it in unexpected measure.

As in life, so in print. The best is free. Still, you may have to pay – directly, for advertising; or indirectly, for someone to prepare your press release; and even better than the best is to be paid for an article which not only advertises your wares, but which can produce reprints, each an invaluable focus for a documentary presentation.

Free print means news value. Editors suffer from chronic shortage of space, but news is the guts of their journals' appeal. From the mighty national to the tiny trade paper, if you provide real news, it will be welcomed. And on the Sam Goldwyn principle that any publicity is good publicity, most editorial comment should be welcomed. Ignorance and silence are the curses of insolvency.

For news and editorial comment, consider two essentials:

- What news can you make, create, organize?
- How do you best spread the word?

As to making news, watch any first-class politician at work. The media wants to headline his efforts on, say, pro-abortion or anti-drug abuse or it-matters-not-what? Then he will find some appropriate Parliamentary or Congressional peg to hang it on – a question, a speech, a motion, or debate. . . .

So can you not open or unveil a new plan, plant or project . . . an extension, promotion or preview? Or maybe an appointment, reorganization or massive review of resources? Then try a press conference to promote news, real or apparent.

Next: the planted story. Your public relations experts should know what to place best – and where, how and through whom. You provide the material at their suggestion. If they cannot suggest, present and place, then you need someone else to replace them and represent you and yours.

Which leaves: articles – and how to place and write them.

Job One: finding your market. As in business, so in the media. The better known you become, the more marketable your produce, and the more thriving the marketplace, the more likely it is that an editor or producer will invite you to appear on his pages or programme. Conversely, the less your renown and the worse the recession or depression, the more you will have to go hunting.

A wit defined the difference between recession, depression and recovery as follows: a recession is when others are out of work; a depression is when you are out of work; recovery is when the government is out of work!

When it comes to placing an article, for most people – private, professional or commercial – the recession and depression are permanent and recovery requires selling which, in its turn, involves the exercise of all those other skills in communication, which this book explains in such detail. These include:

- Study and know your market. Which paper, TV or radio programme or other outlet is likely to use what material and when?
- Who actually controls what goes into the paper or outlet? How can you beam in on that individual to best effect?
- Should you start with a query letter, offering the idea – or kick off with a telephone call, a lunch or a drink?

- Can you respond to a variation on your suggested theme? Are you able to vary your article or idea to the client's requirement, as you would your product or your service?
- Can you meet the likely deadline? Will you need to provide the graphics as well as the text and, if so will you have the appropriate professional help – journalistic or graphic – available in time?
- If your idea is accepted and your material presented, will it be changed or sub-edited ('subbed')? Are you prepared for the likely revision?
- Your article should stress the main points in your message –what are they? And if you are asked for a biography or bibliography, are they available?

Techniques of article writing differ only in degree from those used in the best of letterwriting. Remember especially, though:

- To use, but not to overuse, data, graphs and statistics. An article is meant to be read and reread – usually by people with their feet up at the end of a long hard day. So try to keep down the number of graphs and illustrations.
- To use quotations – but sparingly and accurately and, where possible, with attribution. (You can always say: 'Was it not Oscar Wilde who remarked. . .?' One writer enquired: 'Was it not I who said. . .?')
- Case studies create real situations with which the reader can identify. But if these include references to actual clients or customers, get their consent before using or misusing their good names.

As with letters, so with articles – style counts. Start and end well; structure your sentences and your piece; choose your words with Anglo-Saxon care; avoid the passive, when you can; and do your best to imitate the 'house style' of the journal. Remember: the more your style fits with that of the paper, the less the 'subbing' and the greater your chances not only of publication, but of avoiding the hacking out of those parts which you think the most important, but which the paper may prefer to omit.

So prepare for your market and then organize your mind and your material, before you write. If the material is already on file, perhaps as the basis or in the form of a speech, then knock it into proper form before you ship it out. Few can give the same words the same impact in both forms.

In speech, you have the advantage of vocal and facial expression to illustrate your words. In articles, both are absent. Conversely: with articles, you can place photographs and graphics. Use them.

In speech, a statement may sound humorous and be accepted as such. In an article, the humour may be replaced by offence.

If a book is worth writing, a publisher will normally pay for it. As with books, so with articles. Negotiate your fee in advance. Confirm in writing.

Still: the fee for a presentational article is secondary to your need to get the material into printable or reprintable form. So negotiate accordingly.

The press provides your top potential for communicating with the public. Use it like a professional and it will serve you well.

50

Press Conferences

You may communicate with the press individually or by calling a press conference. Put out news via the Press Association and you can turn an individual moment into a national release. But real publicity for a major story is best achieved by calling the media together. Here are the basic rules on how to do it.

No story should mean no conference. Do not send the troops away without a tale to tell.

To present yourself, your case or your company to one journalist may be difficult. To do so before a press conference could be much worse. You should carefully consider how and when to call each press conference; where and how to run it – and especially how to ensure that it does not ruin you. Let me summarize:

- You start with your story. How do you present it to specialized media – press, radio or television? But if it is major or national . . . if you are creating, building or following up a story of consequence, then you have two likely courses.
- You can contact the Press Association or other national news agency; get them to put the story out over their wires; and wait for the media to come to you. Or you can set up a press conference, itself an event – and yourself invite the media to share the story with you.
- Like any other medium or agency, you may contact the news agency through a reporter with whom you have a special relationship.

Anyway, you can telephone the agency or your local equivalent and ask for the news desk or for a particular department. Or even phone 'copy'. Like any newspaper, the news agencies and wire services employ people who take down 'copy' by telephone.

If using copy, write out your statement in advance. Keep it brief and vivid.

Now assume that you decide to call a press conference. Here are some of the most important rules.

- Choose your time, place and victims with great care – and bring them in by a telephone or written invitation, or by issuing a press release – or both.
- Try to make sure that you have invited the right people. If dealing with the press, check by a telephone call to the editor's secretary – a vital ally – that you have asked the most relevant person.
- Make sure the venue is easily accessible. Journalists have a habit of not turning up if they feel that the journey is too difficult, especially if it rains.
- If a newspaper or journal cannot send a representative, make an appointment to visit its office, leaving a sample and your press kit.
- When dealing with a product or service launch do so well before the launch, but put an embargo date on all material.
- If someone accepts your invitation but does not show up, put your press kit and sample in the post to them that afternoon, so that they can see it the next morning. Then ring them, to make sure that they have received it; if necessary, arrange a visit.
- When dealing with radio and TV, be sure to choose and contact the correct programmes. Titles are sometimes deceptive, so watch or listen to the programmes you intend to contact and note how they present their stories. Bear these presentations in mind when preparing material for them; rewrite as necessary.
- Make contact with the radio or TV programme editor, initially by letter, giving brief details; follow with a telephone call, a few days later. Remember (again): act well in advance if you want the item used on the launch day.
- Radio and TV are often unable or reluctant to use brand names on the air, so make sure that your product is easily identified – even without use of its name.
- When fixing the time of a press conference, check with three or four of the journalists you regard as most important.

Try to ensure that your launch does not clash with anyone else's press conference or reception. Contact your key people first by telephone, to ask if they are able to attend. Ask them to put a pencil note into their diaries, then confirm your telephone conversation by letter and/or by printed invitation, as soon as possible.

- Do not forget that the trade journals are usually weekly, fortnightly or monthly publications and consumer monthly magazines may have as much as a two-month lead-in time between receiving information and printing it. Always find out which day of the week the trade papers go to press or you may find that on your great day the journalists are down at their printers. Once again if necessary, give details in advance, embargoed.

- If you seek maximum attendance, the best time for your conference is between 10.30 a.m. and noon – before 10, the media sleepeth, arouseth and prepareth. After noon, you miss lunchtime TV and the afternoon and evening press. Film for evening TV news bulletins and magazine programmes must be processed and cut; likewise, radio tapes must be edited. So morning conferences are usually best.

- You will need to prepare in advance press kits which will be handed out to your press guests as they arrive and sign themselves into the 'Visitors Book' – a necessary record of attendance.

A press kit must always look professional. You will need a brochure; a press release – about the product or service and possibly about the company or organization; details of other products or services offered; and prices.

Provide if you can a large black and white photograph of the new product with a caption on the back attached securely enough to avoid loss, but not so that the photograph is damaged when it is removed. The photograph should be clear and uncluttered, and printed on glossy paper for best reproduction.

Because you will be giving the journalists several pieces of paper as well as the photograph, enclose them in a strong folder, to avoid loss or damage. If you cannot afford specially printed and made up cardboard folders, use clear plastic.

If you are providing a product sample, you may also need carrier bags. Perhaps your company has stocks of bags already with its own logo? But plain white plastic carriers will do the job.

Journalists are always happy to have a pre-digest of their media meal. So do produce a handout for each arrival, with carefully, prepared, brief and pithy information. The more trouble you save them, the more likely they are to use your material.

Do not – ever – invite the media to receive hard news at your conference and then give one of them the jump on the rest. If you wish, you can mark your press release: 'Embargoed until. . .' That will be honoured.

Journalists are hungrier for news than for sustenance, so there is no need to provide a banquet. If you do, your motives may be suspect. But a cup of hot coffee and biscuits, or a bottle of beer, or a tot of whisky shows a touch of humanity and appreciation at any time. Noon and lunchtime conferences require drinks and sandwiches.

Now suppose that you have gathered your conference. How do you best handle it and present your case? Do not be inflated or deflated by numbers large or small (respectively). Attendance depends upon competing news or its absence that day or hour – over which local politicians, terrorists and other copy-providers have far more influence than your story could ever achieve.

Start with the Chair – preferably someone who knows how to deal with the press.

The Chair should welcome the arrivals; get their names and media origins; pass you a copy, so that you can address them by name – both as a courtesy and so that you can identify the likely bias of your initial audience and of your later questioners; and after opening the proceedings, he should hand them over to the presenter of the case – which we will now presume to be you.

Normally, a press conference need last no longer than about half an hour. Once the formal proceedings are over, individual journalists may wish to ask additional questions privately. Allow them to do so. If radio or TV is represented, the interviewers will want a quiet room or suitable place to operate their magic recording boxes. Make sure that you have one for them.

Whether you are questioned publicly or privately, mind your words. If you need to provide background information or un-attributable details, explain your problems and your wishes will almost invariably be honoured.

Always do a follow-up – a telephone call or a further meeting – with every person to whom you presented your product or service. If you do not chase them up and find out whether the product is going to be mentioned and if not, then why not, all your efforts may die forgotten, buried at the back of someone's filing cabinet.

When all is over, hope for the best. Calling the conference is the beginning; getting people to attend and making your presentation is the middle; but the means only justify the end if and when your news actually appears in print, on radio or on TV.

51

Press Releases

A press release is a document sent out to the press or other medium, setting out what its authors would like others to read or hear about the company or firm, the product or project, the idea or the ideal concerned.

Communication with the press should be preceded by a release; and those attending a press conference should certainly receive one.

Here, then, is your digest of the main rules on the art of releasing your news to the media:

- Before preparing your release, decide to whom it should go, when, and the message you wish to convey.
- Select your recipients with care, otherwise you waste your resources; more important – you misjudge your market.
- Put the release into journalists' language and you vastly enhance its usefulness. Keep it brief; pithy; to the point.
- If all your audiences have the same or similar interests, then one press release will do for the lot. But you cannot use the same press release for both trade and consumer publications. They are two different audiences and need separate releases and possibly even different press conferences. If you combine them at one conference, make sure that the right kit gets to the right journal.
- For a professional release, you will need printed paper with the company logo and 'News Release' printed at the top of the page. You can use ordinary letterheads, but make sure that you include 'News Release' when you print.
- If ordering paper specially, check to see what weight of paper your copier can cope with – usually 80 or 90 gms. Otherwise you may be left with a broken machine and a large pile of scrap paper.
- Date the release – and number it, if applicable. Put an embargo

or release date at the top. Put the heading into capitals and never underline because this would mean in printer's jargon 'print in italics' and could cause confusion.

- Always leave a good space between each line (double spacing on a typewriter) to allow the journalist or sub-editor to alter the release. In that way, your original piece of paper goes right through to the typesetter eliminating the risk of mistakes creeping in, due to the piece having to be retyped. And leave a wide margin on the left for printers' instructions.
- Enclose any correspondence or other documents to which the press release refers.
- Obtain the consent of the writer or author of such documents, if necessary.
- If appropriate, include the name, address and/or telephone number of a contact from whom further information can be obtained.
- Above all: make sure that you meet deadlines – that press releases arrive in good time to be included in issues or editions appropriate to the event. The announcement of a future occasion that has already been held is a certainty for the 'spike' or bin.
- If you send out the wording of a speech to be made in the future, be especially careful with the embargo – and ensure that the speaker follows his script, or otherwise carefully informs those media which have received the prior release of any deviation. And mark the key passages which you hope will be underlined or prominently reproduced.
- When writing the release, headline your message at the start; elaborate it in the middle; and repeat it at the end.
- Recognize that writing a press release requires journalistic expertise. If you do not possess it, yourself or in-house, use a consultant.

52

Microphones and Amplification

Mass communication on even a modest scale means microphones. How then do you best use a microphone and make it your ally?

First, ensure that your mike is switched on. Talk into it. Say:'Can you hear me?' Nothing is more embarrassing than to talk into a dead microphone when you think it is alive but your audience knows that it is not.

Next, adjust the microphone to your height. Whether it is a standing or a table model, you will probably find a turning ring near the centre which, with a combination of luck and some reasonable wrist power, should enable you to fix the mike at just below the level of your mouth. The top of the speaking part of the instrument should be almost level with your lips.

You may be given a neck mike. The engineers will adjust it, for sound and for level.

Position the microphone, even if this means keeping people waiting while you adjust the cord or, if at a table, while it gets lifted over the wine and whisky. With the position and the level right and the mike switched on, you now re-check for volume.

You should be able to stand (or, in some cases, to sit) comfortably and perhaps 6 inches away from the microphone and still have your voice come through loud, clear and undistorted. If there is a scream, a whistle or a shriek, it is on too loud; if a whisper, too soft. If your voice sounds as if it comes from outer space, with Martian echo or eerie ululation, then something needs adjusting.

This, of course, is not an engineer's summary. It is simply the result of years of a love-hate acquaintance with microphones.

So get hold of the mike, position it and speak out. If the sound is wrong, then stop and have it adjusted before you launch into your speech.

Once you are speaking into the mike, remember that usually you are limited in your movement. When you shift away from the mouthpiece, the volume falls. Turn your head either way and your words may be addressed to the entire hall but heard only by those at your feet. Find your distance from the machine and stay there. Within limits, you can relax. But move outside those limits and a lot is lost. Hence, of course, the special virtue of the hanging or neck mike. Use one of them and (assuming as before, that it is properly adjusted) you can move wherever the cord will allow.

For this reason, the neck mike or one that can be unclipped or removed from its stand is better than the fixed, standing variety.

Lift or unclip an ordinary mike off its stand; tuck your elbow into your side; make sure that there is plenty of play in the cord, and walk, keep the mike at the same distance from your mouth.

Communicators who speak into a fixed, standing microphone, then rush across the stage to point silently to some screen and then back to the microphone once more, are asking for trouble. They are also, of course, breaking their thread of speech and the audience's chain of thought. The good speech has continuity. The attention of the audience remains with the words spoken or, at least, with the speakers' thoughts and not with their movements.

Beware of radio microphones. They tend to be unreliable, capricious and liable to outside interference.

Experience will show each communicator how to best make use of the microphone. But most of the above rules apply to us all. Never panic when the amplifier goes wrong. Be prepared to fall back on your own voice power, if you have to – so that you are really not afraid of the microphone giving out.

53

Props

Props – visual aids, samples, documentation, plans or maps – all have their place in the communicator's arsenal. They should be kept in their place. That means:

- Know and understand the nature and purpose of each prop.
- Consider the nature of of the occasion, the participants and the purpose of the communication – and then work out the best props for that occasion and purpose.
- Study and learn the use of the props, so that you handle them professionally and with precision.
- Prepare the props for the occasion, so that they are readily available, easily accessible, in proper order and with all their handlers – yourself, of course, but also (where appropriate sound or other engineers, or additional assistants, or colleagues – know their props and how to use them.

As with the stage, so with communications. Props are vital; if used well, they are a mighty asset and sometimes an essential. Mishandled, misused or fumbled, they fail.

Theatre moments when actors climb battlements which collapse, guns fail to fire, scenery collapses, props disintegrate – these are nightmares.

The theatre – and also, for that matter, films – are, of course, recognized as ancient and modern forms of culture and of communication. Do not forget that any other forms of communication are variants of the theatre. When you lecture, talk in public, pitch or present or speechmake – you are part of the entertainment business. In your own and possibly modest way, you are a performer, writing your own script. You must also have your own appropriate props, which can produce their own equivalent catastrophes. Common examples:

- You step on the cord of your neck mike, which flips onto the ground. You will not enjoy your undignified efforts to pick it up and rehitch it.
- Flip charts collapse. You have not ensured that they were properly footed and well screwed.
- Your overhead or 35mm projector refuses to cooperate. No spare is handy.
- Documents are out of date order, pages are missing, the photocopier has missed out crucial columns or lines.

So let's look at some of the communicator's top props and how to prepare, to handle and to use them.

54

Visual Aids

Words are the essence of communication, but as people learn, understand, absorb messages and are spurred into action by sight as well as by sound, visual aids should be harnessed to assist the communicator. They supplement but never supplant words.

Visual aids add colour, variety and style. They must be selected with care and used with economy and skill. They are essential to modern presentation. They range from the simplicity and immediacy of flip charts to the complexity of computers. In general, we recommend the simple, the available, the flexible, the personal.

Flip charts can be prepared in advance, used at the time or left standing. Make sure that the chart is firmly footed and that your coloured pens or markers are available and have not dried out.

Overhead projectors are admirable, for all visual aid purposes other than the projection of pictures, photographs or of some plans or graphs. Transparencies should be concise, compact and uncluttered, using abbreviations and symbols to summarize and emphasize, and art work sparingly and for results, not effect.

Wording should be kept to a sensible minimum. Visual aids must not be allowed to replace your verbal message. They provide the skeleton, attracting the eye and directing the mind. Complication should be communicated in accompanying documents. We recommend also that you supply copies of the charts or transparencies to your delegates, so that they can watch and listen without deflecting their concentration into writing or copying.

Slides should have clear, light backgrounds and dark, brisk lettering. 'Funnies' are too often wet. Oral humour is better and, if it fails, ephemeral.

Choose your projectors and other machinery with care, the more soundless, the better. We keep a reserve machine available in case the first breaks down.

To point at a transparency, use a pencil on the slide itself. Keep it still. Or use the shadow of your pointed finger. Never allow the shadow of your body to be cast on the screen.

Changes of transparency should be slick. Hold the replacement in your right hand; remove the existing transparency with your left and put the new one in its place, all in one movement; and practise until you can put the replacement into a firm, central position, without fiddling.

Be deliberate in your movements; use variety in your charts, different types, colours, underlining. Do not talk while you change transparencies or slides. And always remember to keep visual aids to the minimum.

These rules are even more important, when applied to 35 mm slide presentations. Problems of slides include inflexibility; difficulty in pointing to the screen; but above all, the removal of attention from the communicator, in a room which must be at least partially darkened. Advantages: if well prepared, the slides present the word in pictures. We recommend: use of slides where necessary, but not throughout the presentation. The relationship between the communicator and the audience matters most. Hide yourself in darkness and you cannot excel.

So why not tell the tale first? Use overheads for illustration. Then sum up with your slides?

Or set the scene with the slides at the start and close it with others at the end? Just as the skilled speaker will vary tone, pace and content to attract and to keep the attention of his audience, so he will use a variety of visual aids, to suit his occasion and purpose.

Then there are audio cassettes. In the USA, this medium is far more developed than in the UK. Many companies, including our own, have marketed audio cassettes, for training or instruction. Most (like ours) have ruefully decided that Britons prefer other methods.

Still, there is nothing to prevent you from communicating by tape, if you have an audience which will be prepared to listen.

Videos have their own impact. They can be seen privately on a small screen or publicly on a large one, they can convey a message with clarity. But they must be professionally prepared, at a heavy cost.

When considering a video presentation, then, bring in the experts. You will find that their approach and their quotes are amazingly varied.

Finally: the computer. When properly harnessed and carefully programmed and used, computers may help explain complex ideas, especially to tutored minds. Too often, though, the audience is captivated by the genius of the medium, rather than by the sight of the message. Avoid it, except for special occasions and after special training.

When asked for his view on a potentially dangerous opponent, a wise politician replied, 'My motto with him is: Respect and suspect.'

Treat modern technology as an adjunct to personal presentation with respect and with suspicion – and with the help of experts. It is no amateur game. Training and instruction are as vital to communications as they are to any other area of expertise.

55

Outdoor Communication

Outdoor communications range from the simplicity of a loud-speaker to the sophistication of portable exhibitions – from skywriting by aircraft to advertising by balloon.

Mobile loudspeakering is an election essential and an advertising occasional. If you wish to use a speaker to advertise an event, check on local byelaws.

The more powerful your loudspeaker, the greater its likely effect. Hand-operated machines are fine if you are talking from the roof or the back of your vehicle to a throng of listeners, but they are useless on the move.

Use the best equipment and you can whisper into the loud-speaker and boom your message literally through the walls of houses. The techniques are simple but vital.

Keep your message extremely brief; pronounce each word separately and clearly; keep your batteries charged and your equipment guarded; and make sure that you have an experienced driver to steer the vehicle out of trouble, leaving you to concentrate on the loudspeaker.

Outdoor presentations require specialized planning, equipment and techniques. Gripping and holding an audience out of doors is almost always more challenging than inside. Move acoustics outside a room, hall or building and they become both worse and different.

Historians and playwrights have created epic speeches, delivered to packed and enraptured multitudes, everywhere from Mount Sinai to Plymouth Hoe – but have you ever wondered how anyone managed to hear them? Ancient prophets and medieval kings may have had mighty lungs, but none could match even the most miserable of loudspeakers.

If you are speaking out of doors to any more than a handful of folk, make sure of your equipment. If it fails, so will you. Take care, too, that it is well sited. Light reflects and sound bounces.

56

Communicating by the Book

For me, to write good fiction is impossible. Years ago, I wrote the first few chapters of a political murder, entitled 'Candidate for Death'. I sent them to my literary agent, who wrote back: 'My Dear Greville. Your title was excellent. But I hope you will not be hurt if I suggest that you stick to writing about law, or some other subject about which you are knowledgeable.'

That ended my fiction writing. Which is perhaps just as well. Out of the (literally) tens of thousands of novels written each year in the English language, only a small percentage are published. Of those published, only a few make money. Of those few, only the tiniest fraction become best sellers.

Whether you write fact or fiction, if the book is worth publishing someone will bear the cost. If you are asked to pay for the publication, then unless you are either very rich or desperate to see your words in print or able to find some angel or organization to sponsor your work, decline, firmly and finally.

How, then, is a book written? Authors' methods and routines are as varied as the writers and their subjects. For fiction, you will probably need to follow your story from day to day, retaining the train and the trail, the characters and their moods and actions, clearly in mind. You may set aside hours for writing, tying yourself to table, typewriter or word processor. If you wait until the spirit moves you, you may lose your deadline.

Deadline? That is the date by which the manuscript must be delivered. Most writers need deadlines. Most contracts provide them.

Contracts? Your publishers will produce their 'standard documents' and invite you to believe that they are as immutable as the tablets of stone, consigned to Moses on Mount Sinai.

It is told of a certain Cabinet Minister that he was sent by his Prime Minister back to the sacred mountain, to renegotiate the Ten

Commandments. On his return he gathered his colleagues about him: 'My dear friends,' he said. 'I have done as the Boss hath commanded. Do you wish first to hear the good news or the bad news?'

'Tell us the bad news, the bad news,' his colleagues clamoured.

'The bad news is that I have been unable to get rid of the one about adultery,' he said.

'And the good news, the good news?'

'The good news is that there are still only ten!'

There may be only ten 'standard forms' of publishers' contracts, but each one of them is negotiable. As in all business matters, the negotiators' success will depend upon their strength and the skill with which they wield it. The most crucial question: How much does the publisher want you on its list? If the answer is 'Not much', then you are probably stuck with the standard deal. If (as in my happy case) the choice of publishers is essentially mine, then negotiations are open. Consider:

- The advance – how much you will be paid in advance, and by what instalments. You can expect a third on signature, a third on acceptance of manuscript and the balance on publication.
- The royalty. What percentage of the selling price will you receive? While advances are useful to keep the bank manager happy, in the long run it is the royalty that should count. It is rarely worth selling all your rights, just in case your book takes off.
- Rights. You are, of course, selling the right to publish the book. But in which country or countries? And what about serial rights – or film or TV rights?
- Author's copies. The contract will probably provide for six. You could always ask for two dozen. If your family or friends do not demand them, then you can sell them.
- The liabilities. Watch out for libel and for copyright. Will you need insurance?
- Deadline. By all means put yourself under pressure, but do not make commitments that you cannot honour.

What then, of the writing itself? For me, there is only one essential instrument: a dictating machine.

Some authors draft their words in long hand. Others sit at their word processors, tapping out their masterpieces. For me, words flow better from the mouth and into a machine.

Whatever your method, there are days when your words will cascade, and others when the spirit runs dry.

My creative hours are the first in any day. When in the mood, the flow is a pleasure.

One fabulous summer's morning by a lake in Canada, my wife sat watching as I walked by the water, chatting into my machine. 'Can't you ever stop working?' she enquired, gently.

'It isn't work,' I replied. 'If your husband enjoyed painting and sat by a lake with his canvas and palette and brushes, would you accuse him of workaholism? Well, for me there is a delight in putting ideas into balanced prose – provided that I am not under pressure of time.'

If you have a book in you, then you should enjoy writing it. And if that book is non-fiction, it should write itself.

Keep a notebook with you. Or dictate ideas for stories, jokes, witticisms, articles or chapters onto your pocket machine. The book will grow.

As the articles, the chapters and the notes pile one on the other, the book expands.

Lay out your chapters on floor or table. Scribble missing chapter headings on blank paper. Slot the lot together and beat out your contents and (if the book is still to be sold) your synopsis. Then you are off.

There is no book more beautiful than your first. But just as each baby born is lovelier than the last, so you will take pride in each book as it is born.

57

Tell Them a Story

Every parent knows that every child loves a story. But too many forget too often that adults also wish to be entertained; and the more talented the communicator, the greater the content of anecdote, parable or illustration in the message.

In New York, I listened to a skilled financial consultant, explaining complex problems of mortgage planning, networked by television, from coast to coast. He began by summing up what he was going to say. 'Today, it will be my pleasure to explain to you some methods which I have evolved, which could save you thousands of dollars, when you take out a mortgage.' Then back to the studio audience: 'On the principle that $10,000 saved – after the tax man has done his worst – will be at least $20,000 earned – is there anyone here who would *not* like to save $10,000, literally without effort? Well, is there? Of course not. So let me tell you how. . . .'

Then the performer – for that is what he was – threw some brisk, simple statements to the screen, and explained them. 'That's the guts of the matter,' he said. 'Now let me show you how it works.' Then the story:

'I have a friend called Bill, who is in a small way of business. He's married with a couple of young kids. He phoned me last week and he asked, "Tell me, Joe, what are the best ways of getting a mortgage on the most sensible terms?" So I told him.'

Joe then explained his schemes in ordinary language, just as he would have done to his friend. No lecture, no jargon, but instead a story, with a happy ending.

'Yesterday, Bill phoned me and told me that by following my advice, he had got just the mortgage he wanted and at a very substantial saving.'

With practice, you can weave stories in and out of any present-ation. Suppose, for instance, that you are introducing a proposal to prospective customers. You would expect to illustrate with graphs, figures or photographs, depending on the subject? Then why not also explain through the experience of others who have used your methods or products?

Instead of simply introducing colleagues by name and job description, tell of their exploits. 'Mary is in charge of the public relations side of a similar operation. By the simple expedient of . . . she threw the whole set up into marvellous relief, capturing columns of editorial content, all of it favourable. As an example. . . .'

'Martin looks after the European end of our business. He set up the conference in . . . where the Minister of . . . seized the idea, recommended it to his State undertakings, with the result that. . . .'

Nor need you leave parables to those who so successfully marketed the world's great religions. 'Did you hear the story about . . . Well, it may be apocryphal but it does show clearly, doesn't it, that . . .'

Part VI

SOME FINAL THOUGHTS

58

Learning to Communicate

Your brain operates every moment you are alive – except when you get onto your feet to make a presentation or otherwise to communicate in public. Professionals in the field have learned to overcome this handicap, while amateurs need expert training.

Basic oral communication begins with a baby's first signals and continues until the dying breath. The extent and usefulness of that communication depends to some extent on the individual's native intelligence and intellect, but equally on training and acquired expertise.

A researcher was asked to find out why it is that where two children are born with equal intelligence, one grows up with a bleak vocabulary of a few hundred words, while the other becomes a skilled communicator. She told the following story:

'Johnny is sitting on a bus with his mother. She says to him, "Sit back." He says, "Why?" She replies, "Because I say so."'

'Mary is on the same bus. Her mother says, "Sit back." She says, "Why?" Her mother replies, "Because if you do not, the bus will stop suddenly and you will be thrown forward and will hurt yourself."'

'Is it any wonder that Johnny's talents develop less than Mary's?'

Another example, from my own constituency. I often go to assemblies in primary schools. If I ask the children in a well off area, 'When do you eat with your Mum and Dad or whoever you live with?' The answer is, 'Every day.' In the disadvantaged areas, the answer is often, 'Only on Sundays, for dinner.' This means that once a week, on Sundays, at midday, they sit as a family – and chat, discuss, argue and even row.

Is it any wonder, then, that those who communicate early and at home sharpen their vocabularies, their words and their tongues better than those who effectively communicate only with others at their own level of linguistic achievement? And so on through the generations. . . .

What, then, of learning by television? The box spews out a rich variety of words. So why do those children who sit glued to the object for an average of 4–8 hours a day, emerge with a tiny vocabulary. If communication before them is so filled with vivid wording, why is their own so poor?

Teachers tell us that people learn through participation. Television in schools is the basis for discussion. Put youngsters before a screen and they will see and understand much but learn little.

So to learn your own language, you must use it. That use requires training, which may be homely and informal or skilled and expert, depending upon its nature and requirement.

Now apply the same rules to language used to communicate with those who speak in different tongues. But (as Jonathan Swift remarked): 'Proper words in proper places, make the true definition of a style'. It is hard enough choosing those 'proper words' in your own language, but far harder in other people's.

Languages must be learned. The best way to learn to communicate with others is to have no alternative. As a youngster, I learned several languages by working among children who spoke no English but only the language that I wanted to acquire. For instance, I taught English in a village school in Spain, by what was known as 'the direct method' – through gesture and through song. The children taught me Spanish through interminable games of Pelota and chess.

The alternative is to take lessons. You could use tapes or records, but class or (better still) individual coaching is better and quicker.

Communication, then, must be taught. Learning requires enough humility to recognize that you need it.

If you are not satisfied with your own level of expertise in communication, how do you acquire it? The equivalent of learning language through talking is having work experience. If, as is likely, you have work which does not provide the experience, then you must seek teaching. But before you start, consider the following questions:

● What do you want to learn? What are your specific requirements or those of your colleagues? This includes: To what use will you put your skill when you have acquired it?

　　For instance: It is not enough to decide that you would like to communicate on your feet. Are you concerned primarily with addressing public meetings; talking to your own board, to your colleagues, to your work force; to customers or to clients, actual or potential? Or are you more interested in (for instance) selling? Do you simply want confidence? Or are you worried by a stammer or other speech defect?

- Who provides the sort of training that you require, where, when and at what cost?
- Which of the possible training organizations or individual trainers will best suit your perceived need?
- How should you best winnow down the possibles? Can you get brochures, details, quotations and, above all, recommendations and references, from previous clients?
- Should you set up a beauty contest, to see how each presents – and then decide among the possibles by (perhaps) organizing a trial or a pilot session?

There are now many organizations who teach communication and presentation skills. They vary widely in their areas and levels of expertise. Some, for instance, specialize in personal communication; others in television or radio. Some are skilled at the top and some at every level. What do you need and how can you ensure that it is satisfied?

So start by recognizing your requirements, then meet them. Communication without training should be (as Michael Foot once said of 'military intelligence') a contradiction of terms!

59

To Be Or Not To Be (There)

A visiting American telephoned the parish Church in Sandringham, where the Royal Family were on holiday. 'Will Their Royal Highnesses be in church this Sunday?' the voice enquired.

'That we cannot promise,' replied the vicar. 'But we confidently expect God to be there, and we hope that will be incentive enough to a reasonably large attendance!'

In your business, you may be God. But you are not omnipresent. Like the Royal Family itself, you must consider for each occasion whether it requires your personal presence and if not, then whether you should be represented by a substitute and if so, then who.

There are two types of occasion which you may attend, those to which you are invited and others which you yourself create.

Survival requires your ruthless culling of invitations. The greater your celebrity, the more careful that culling must be.

Some invitations take obvious care of themselves. There are those that are inescapable: general meetings of companies; absolute demands from superiors with power; subpoenas from courts or their commercial equivalents. These you accept, diary and prepare to meet.

Others are obviously inessential and, however worthy, a use of time which you cannot spare. These are refused, promptly and with courtesy (see also Chapter 26 on Refusals).

In any case of doubt, consult — at work, a trusted colleague, as you would at home, your spouse.

When elected President of a large and busy organization, I set up an apparently simple criterion, for the Secretary-General's consideration. 'The question is not whether Greville Janner should attend,' I told him. 'It is whether the occasion is one which requires the presence of the President. If it is, he goes. If not, he does not and we decide whether or not we seek a substitute.'

Depersonalize your response to official invitations. Ask yourself and your colleagues, 'Does the occasion or the audience demand or merit the attendance of the Chief Executive, Managing Director, Personnel Chief'. And as you cannot necessarily stand back from yourself to judge your own importance or (especially) your lack thereof, share the decision. Considerations should include:

- The size, importance and power of the audience and, in particular
- whether the audience or anyone in it will decide on matters of real importance to you or to your business, your enterprise or your function.
- Whether you have a moral obligation to attend — perhaps to help a small or ailing but worthy organization — or to oblige a colleague, or to disarm your critic, in particular
- whether if you do not go, you or your company or organization will be in trouble.
- Whether your audience or the gathering would be prepared to accept a substitute and if so, then at what level — and is there one available?

A leading politician accepted an invitation to give an after dinner speech. He was forced to cancel, due to an important vote in the House. He wrote to apologize, profoundly and sincerely.

The host of the evening telephoned in anguish, 'What do we do?' he wailed. 'Can you please look for a substitute. And we need someone like you — someone who is a wit.'

Gravely, the MP replied, 'I will gladly look for a substitute,' he said. 'I'm not sure, though that I can find you a wit. But I think I could fill your bill with two people whom I know. They could both come. And each of them is a half wit!'

If substitute there must be, select with care. Just as General Douglas McArthur remarked that 'in war, there is no substitute for victory', so in communication there is not necessarily any substitute for you. Still, look and you never know your luck.

As a start, if a speaker is not vital at your level, then perhaps you could send your deputy, assistant or senior colleague or employee. Clearly, you must choose someone who will present your excuses in the proper manner and not use the occasion to undermine your position or authority. More constructively, it could provide experience and exposure for someone who either needs or would appreciate both.

Your substitute could give or (better) read a brief message from you. Or if you are sufficiently mighty, you could supplement his or heı presence by a video presentation. If your company has its own equipment and expertise, this need not be as expensive as it sounds.

I once attended a talk given by a local vicar at an institution for delinquent boys. 'My theme,' he said, 'is simple. If you are going to do a job, you should do it properly.' The audience roared its approval.

If you are making a video presentation, then that, too, is better done well or not at all. Usually, it is only worth spending time and resources if it can promote your message, many times over.

The ultimate question in each case, though, remains, must or should you make the communication in person?

The ultimate compliment — 'He took the trouble to speak to us himself.' The converse — 'He did not even trouble to talk to us. He sent his minion.'

So decide on whether or not to accept an invitation. If you refuse, consider a substitute. And make sure that any you provide is appropriate.

Samuel Goldwyn once employed a ghostwriter to produce a series of articles, to be published under his name. When the job was half done, the ghostwriter fell ill. A substitute took over. When Goldwyn read one of his pieces, he cried out in anguish, 'That's not up to my usual standard!' he proclaimed.

Your substitutes must be up to your usual standard, or you will rightly be blamed.

60

Do You Read Me?

To read is not the same as to read well. But it is at least a start. Benjamin Franklin was right, 'The condition of man most deserving pity,' he said, 'is a lonely man on a rainy day who does not know how to read.'

All business people write communications to others and must read those directed at them. To this there is a lost art, worth reacquiring.

You could begin by smashing your TV set. Or banish it to some part of your home that you do not inhabit. If your children are to be as illiterate as you will be if you were a postwar child, then let them view while you read. Better still: incur their dire wrath by donating the oblong object to your neighbours. You may occasionally lose sight of your children, but that will help ensure the tranquillity which reading require ..

The only true pa..n to reading skills, then, is simply: to read. Voraciously, widely, intelligently, but almost anything is better th..n nothing. In the process, not only will your appetite grow, but so will your own skill in writing.

Not for ordinary mortals the famous dictum of Disraeli, asked what he had recently read. He replied, 'Whenever I wish to read a book, I write one!' Writing and reading are Siamese twins. Together they live; separate them and either may wither.

Unhappily, there is much difference between business reading, and reading at leisure, for pleasure. For enjoyment, it is fine to follow the advice of William Walker, writing in the seventeenth century on *The Art of Reading*. 'Learn to read slow,' he said. 'All other graces will follow in their proper places.' For most of us, there is simply no time for the leisurely reading of business reports, documents, letters and the like, even if we have a masochistic appetite for such pursuits. So swift reading is essential.

For most of us, it takes an effort to learn. So I once joined two of my staff at a course on fast reading.

For six evenings, we sat in front of *Three Men In A Boat*, a novel by Jerome K Jerome, which I had not even enjoyed when I read it slowly. We learned to run our eyes ever faster down the page, as cruel markers forced us steadily ahead.

The result for me: when I returned to ordinary reading — business or pleasure — I was done. Instead of the happy reading of light works which I had all my life enjoyed, I was constantly conscious of the mechanics of the operation. Instead of that careful but swift scanning of documents, which every young barrister learns for survival, I kept thinking not only of the three men in the boat, but also of their wretched dog, whom I would willingly have drowned.

My assistants were rather luckier. One was delighted with the course and maintains that it cured his slow reading. The other shrugs and says, 'I don't suppose it did me any harm.' It took me about two years to get back to my previous prowess.

So by all means learn to read faster and to scan more swiftly. But take care before you plunge into formal lessons.

As a postgraduate student at Harvard Law School, I laughed at the course at Harvard College, entitled 'Reading'. By the time youngsters get to college, I thought, they should at least be literate. I was wrong. The time to study reading skills is the same as the best age to learn to work a computer — as young as possible. A huge percentage of British executives who should know better how to read, do not. It may be never too late to learn, but make sure that the method applied suits you.

Now suppose that you have to cope with business documents; that you do not have time to read them at leisure; and that you find them hard to absorb, especially at speed. The secret lies in swift repetition.

The first time you read the document, absorb the general sense. Next time, look for the key details and try to understand and to absorb them. Then reread, to satisfy yourself that you understand what the reader sought to communicate.

Use precisely the same method for figures. Run your eyes down the balance sheet, profit and loss account, the costing of the project, or whatever. Remember: it is in the long run both quicker and more efficient to scan or read a complex document three times than it is to plod through only once.

Some quick absorbers make jottings or notes as their reading proceeds, and (assuming that the document is not a top copy, to be kept pristine), they underline, highlight, arrow or notate. If you can resist the temptation, it is better to do your jottings on a separate sheet on the first scan and not to mark the document itself until the second time round. By then, your view as to which of the points are especially important or requiring elaboration or emphasis or change may itself have altered.

Of course, if you have the intellect and skills of Isaiah Berlin or of Albert Einstein, you can ignore this advice. If you are blessed with a mind that absorbs complexities through the eyes, at speed and without problems, you are fortunate and if you are not reaching towards the peak of executive success, you will be, should be or have already attained it.

Finally: If all else fails, find consolation in the words of William Hazlitt, 'It is better to be able neither to read nor write than to be able to do nothing else!'

61

Interviews For Office

A multitude of bodies — political, religious, communal, charitable, public or private — interview candidates for office. The fact that the job may be unpaid and fulfilling rather than financially rewarding, in no way removes the potential stress of the interview. So in case you must face this common ordeal, here are some suggestions on the best ways to win. And if you are a group interviewer, stand the hints on their heads and you may reach into some of the realities of your applicants.

First question: Is the job really desirable? How far are the applicants selling themselves, how far are the offerees desperate for even one vaguely qualified aspirant?

The queue of would-be Members of Parliament is never ending. First stage: to get on to the short list of prospective candidates for a winnable (or better still) safe seat.

There is a vintage and, I am assured, entirely true story concerning the death of a veteran Labour MP. The next day, a young aspirant for the vacant seat telephoned the then Secretary of the Party, Ron Hayward.

'I'm so sorry that old Jack has passed away,' he said. 'What are the chances of my taking his place?'

'Well, I don't know,' Ron replied. 'But if the undertaker has no objection, I certainly have none!'

The first question for the applicant, then, whose place are you seeking to take? Once you know, check with his or her supporters. How strong are they and what can you do or say which is likely to put or to keep them on your side? Research into the record, attitudes, successes and failures of the previous incumbent. Ask — yourself and trusted others: What can you do to fill the worthy shoes and to avoid the errors?

Next: who were and are the opponents of the predecessor? 'Sus out' their personalities, strengths and weaknesses, their hopes and their hates. Are they or any of them likely to be your allies? What aspects of your record, programme or approach are most likely to appeal to them, and which will condemn you to their opposition?

Essentially, you are doing your market research. No business people in their right minds will launch a product without first testing the market. Before you head into any interview, you must try to find out what the interviewers are likely to want. At best, you will increase your chances of making a favourable impression; at worst, you may decide to back off, and to waste neither your time nor theirs. Conversely, as an interviewer, you are unlikely to be impressed by an applicant who has not bothered to find out at least the basics of the job, along with the requirements of those who can deliver it.

Next questions: do you lobby your interviewers? Should you canvass individuals or interest groups and if so, how?

Some selection meetings (by whatever name) are effectively sewn up in advance. The contenders and the selectors can preassess the result, within perhaps a vote or two either way. Others are far more open.

One delight of democracy, at least for those who are not wound up in it, is the uncertainty of most of its results. Opinion polls are so often wrong. Votes are only counted when they are in the ballot box.

Assuming, then, that there is neither custom, nor rule to forbid, nor a bias against individual canvassing, pre-interview lobbying is certainly sensible. Most people are flattered to be approached for their view and for their support. 'At least he took the trouble to come and see me. . . .' Some are positively put off by not being approached. 'She never even bothered to canvass me. . . .'

So prepare yourself for your ordeal, by researching both the job and the interviewers. Treat the occasion and the interviewers with respect. Seek and follow the best advice that you can get as to how to put yourself and your case. Then into battle you go.

Naturally, you do all you can to make sure that your backers turn up. Who should telephone whom? Will Mrs Brown need a baby-sitter or old Mr Black a lift to the meeting? Wise applicants leave as little as possible to fickle chance.

Then comes the interview itself. Methods of approach are as varied as the sessions themselves. But the basic rules on present-ation are the same as those for any other interview. For instance:

- Recognize that you are bound to be nervous but conceal your nerves — by standing or sitting straight and with authority . . . by pausing with a smile, before you begin . . . by sparing a few sentences to greet and make contact with your audience . . . and above all, by making and keeping eye contact with your interviewers. . . .

- Watch your timing with care. If, for instance, you are to have ten minutes to present your case, followed by another ten to answer questions, do not risk being cut off during your peroration or before you have made your main points. Time is the enemy and for the interviewee, it passes faster than expected.
- Make, keep and use sensible notes, preferably on cards which can be shuffled, used and discarded. Never, ever, read your presentation.
- Prepare for questions by running over the probabilities with your allies. Do not despise 'the plant'. Encourage your friends to ask the questions which you wish to answer, not only so as to provide you with your platform but so as to block off the time which would otherwise be available for queries which you would prefer to avoid.

Above all: talk to your audience, with understanding and with respect. If you talk down to them, you will lose. If you tread on their susceptibilities, you do not deserve to win.

When I was originally interviewed for selection as Labour candidate for what was then Leicester North West, one of my opponents was an extremely well known television interviewer for a weekly documentary extravaganza. He turned out to be much better at asking questions than at answering them.

'What makes you think that you would be a particularly good candidate for this constituency?' someone enquired.

'I am very well known here,' he said. 'as I am throughout the country. After all, once a week I come into the drawing room of almost every intelligent family.'

The poor man was finished. As a start, most of the people present did not watch his programme and were not particularly flattered to be excluded from the ranks of the intelligent. And anyway, they all had kitchens, bedrooms and living rooms — but drawing rooms? The man might do very well in an interview for some other post, in another time or place. But that answer pronounced the death sentence on his current chances. I was much relieved.

62

Audience Feedback

Communication means the transfer of ideas; the removal of barriers. To discover whether your communication has reached its target, feedback and follow-up are essential.

Start by removing physical barriers. Chatting to an audience from behind a table? Then move around it, if necessary, unhitching the microphone and taking it with you.

You may sit behind your desk to discipline or dismiss. To create informality and mutuality, you will sit alongside your visitor. Transfer this sensible, human arrangement into the hall or onto the platform and you will unite your audience, with nothing to lose but your distance.

Next: relate to them. Start with the word 'you' and keep coming back to it. By all means speak in the first person. The use of 'one' ('one' does, 'one' thinks, 'one' is pleased to be here . . .) is fine in French, but contrived in English. But the vertical pronoun should be spoken with discretion. Concentrate instead on the three letter word: you.

For true long distance communication, the barriers are down. When we visit my wife's family in Australia, direct flying time is about one day. When my wife's mother travelled to the same place some fifty years ago, the journey took seven weeks. We can now dial straight through to her home within seconds. We take telephones for granted. A generation ago, they scarcely existed. Add telex, fax, television and the age of the satellite, and international barriers have disappeared. So do not recreate them, when you communicate in person.

Eye contact is the key. Watch your audience and their reactions. All the time. Then you can:
- Establish your relationship and create your atmosphere.
- Bring expression through your face into your voice.

- Check, all the time, to see how your listeners are reacting to your words, your style, your message — and be ready to change approach, rhythm, style or emphasis, when you see that your current tack is not getting across.

A politician once declaimed, 'We're doing well, lads. From here on up, it's all downhill!' Communications, like cars, have their ups and downs. But if you are not watching the road, you cannot decide on the correct gear. And just as all skilled drivers operate by instinct and habit, their eyes are on the road at all times, ready to switch on their minds at any hint of trouble. As you learn to watch your audience and to accept the feedback from it, so you will soon instinctively match your reactions to those of your listeners.

Because repetition is a vital part of the communicator's art, you will forgive me for repeating that successful communications move in more than one direction. If you do not stop, look and listen for the reactions of your audience, you will fail. Monologues are for Shakespeare. Good speakers share ideas.

What, then, are the techniques for gauging feedback, once you have submitted 'eye' for 'I'? Try the following:

- Most bright people do better in answering questions than in straight speaking. By all means leave plenty of time for questions and comment at the end of your presentation. But in appropriate places (which include most informal occasions and many expositions), why not intersperse questions, to brighten your talk? If I am lecturing, or explaining the law, I always stop after every section or portion where there is a natural break. 'Any questions so far, please? Anything that I have not made clear? Anyone want to comment on . . . ?'
- Defer to and flatter a listener by saying, 'Now, I know that this problem affects your operations, Mr Brown. Can you help us with any further suggestions?' Or, 'Mary, this is your territory. Have I covered it as you would want or would you like to add anything at this stage?'
- If you see someone looking quizzical or pained, beam in. 'Don't you agree with that?' Or, 'Have I not made my point clear enough? I'm sorry. Let me try again. . . .'

Watch out for:

- People whose attention is wandering — especially if they are talking amongst themselves. Walk up to them, look at them, and wait.
- Sleepers and yawners. The Duke of Salisbury is said to have

dreamed that he was speaking in the House of Lords. When he woke up, he found that he was! Politicians were once defined as people who talk while other people are sleeping. Communicators keep both themselves and their audiences well awake — by removing the barriers between them and by watching and listening for and reacting to their audiences, with skill, humour and good nature.

63

Time Savers

Communicators are busy people who should know that the best way to save time is to use it twice. Double time means doing two jobs at the same time. Most meetings are ideal for that purpose.

If, for instance, you have papers to sort, to check through or to sign, why not put them into a briefcase and take them with you to your next, required but essentially boring gathering? Place yourself at the back or at the end of a row, as inconspicuously as possible and surrounded by the maximum space. Listen in to the proceedings with both ears and an occasional eye. Then use the rest of your concentration on the papers which you would otherwise have to peruse and deal with at some other time.

How can you concentrate on two things at once? Easily. The mind is an expandable instrument, seldom fully used.

Consider how often you have been driving your car when you suddenly realize that you have unconsciously travelled a considerable distance. As an experienced driver, the slightest incident on the road would have rivetted your attention to the road. Meanwhile, an important part of your mind was on business, family, pleasure or some other pursuit.

I am not — repeat not — recommending that you should think of something else while driving. All your concentration should be on the road. I merely point out that often it is not. You still get where you are going because your mind is not fully occupied with one pursuit.

The system of using your mind twice is worthy of deliberate practice. Just as few of the speeches at most meetings deserve total attention and concentration, so the same applies to most of your papers. If that portion of your mind which is attending to the meeting flames with the warning that someone is making an important point, then you abandon your papers and concentrate wholly. Equally, if you come across a paper that requires full concentration, you put it to one side for later attention.

For me, working at meetings is not a particular pleasure. It also attracts some unfavourable comment. But as the alternative is to work even further into the early hours of the following day, and as I have to spend so much time at meetings to which and at which I must attend in case of trouble, rather than to play a continuous part, double time used is single time saved.

A warning: if you are chairing a meeting or are actively involved in matters under discussion or if the meeting is small and any lack of apparent attention could be harmful or misunderstood, then keep your eyes, your ears and your attention fixed on the speaker, the Chair and the matter in hand. Otherwise, though, cultivate the art of double time and you will have more moments of precious life left for business, pleasure or (in my case) sleep!

64

Family Festivities

There is no ordeal more potentially horrific than addressing a family gathering. Fumble a speech in Parliament — and which MP has not? — and your catastrophe will soon be overtaken by someone else's. Compared to relatives, political opponents are forgiving and friendly. Mess up a family festivity and the memory of the elephant will be as nothing compared to that of your tribe.

So consider, how can you cope with your 'few remarks' to your family mafia? Here are some basic rules hammered out on my own family anvil.

First: prepare. Far from taking a family audience for granted, recognize it as the enemy it could be. Work out your plan of attack, and put it on to notes.

Then, names. When making any speech, write the names to be mentioned, large and clear. An undistinguished and eminently forgettable politican was once introduced at the Cambridge Union as follows. 'Mr Brown's name is a household word — in his own household!' Watch out for the names in your own household or you could be in terrible trouble.

Presiding at a Christening? Then is the child Carol or Caroline — or, perhaps, Charles, Carl or Carlos? If the groom's name is Michael, does he like being referred to as Mike, Mick or Mickey?

Next: list all those who must be mentioned. Leave anyone out and you will not be forgiven. My wife and I remember the wedding, a quarter century ago, when — in error — the groom did not mention his parents. The only way to avoid this fate is to take notes against it.

Then: jokes. Families love humour, provided, in general, that it is at someone else's expense. So avoid jokes about your parents or grandparents, your children or siblings, your uncles, aunts, cousins or other relatives within what lawyers call the prohibited degrees of consanguity. Which leaves, as joke fodder, only yourself. As in all other gatherings, you may readily laugh at your own expense and expect others to join in.

There are exceptions: like Uncle John, aged 90, who likes to be congratulated on his appetite for women. But even then, I heard a speaker die on his feet at a recent party to celebrate an 80th birthday, killed off by the crudity of his jokes about the birthday boy.

Individual meetings in the company of a parent require understanding from both. My wife and I do our best not to embarrass our own children too greatly through their having to introduce us to their friends.

The rules of non-embarrassment apply on a grander scale to those horrendous occasions when we are called upon to address the family. The beloved mob sit smiling cynically, waiting for the brick to drop. There are no prophets in their own household, no orators in their own families.

When a convicted villian was asked by the judge what he had to say before sentence was pronounced upon him, he replied, 'For Gawd's sake, keep it short!' No greater virtue has a family oration than its brevity.

As with every other presentation, spend a little time making contact with your audience. Relax them with an opening joke. As Henry VIII said to each of his wives in turn, 'Don't worry. I shall not keep you for long!' But the trouble with jokes *en famille* is that the mob will have heard them all. Your husband or wife may smile dutifully, as when greeting a familiar if seedy acquaintance. The rest of the audience are under no such duty. Inwardly, or (more disturbingly) outwardly, they groan. 'There he goes again. . . .'

So do not spend too long on the *hors d'ouevre*. Get stuck into the meal. Bless the child christened or confirmed, the bride and the groom united, the uncle celebrating his ancient birthday ('May he live to 120 and beyond . . .').

Transmit your message (whatever it may be) with courtesy and with wit. Speak well of the living and never, ever criticize the dead.

Some Greek villagers still dig up the skulls of deceased relatives and friends and use them in macabre family festivities, as wine cups to toast the departed. But those who speak ill of the dead are enjoined to keep their lips sealed; and those who think ill of the deceased are forced to keep away.

So if you deliver an obituary at a wake or a memorial, or are required publicly to regret those relatives who are absent through death, either speak well of them or decline to speak at all.

'What a lovely man my husband was,' the widow boasted to a friend. 'You know what I found after Fred died? I opened the safe and there was a big packet, wrapped in brown paper and addressed to me. I opened it and it contained £100,000 in cash!'

'Really,' said the friend. 'Your husband was a saint.'

'But that wasn't all. There were three more packets, one addressed to each of the children. And each contained £25,000 in cash!'

'What a marvellous man he was.'

'And there was even another packet. A small one. Addressed to me. It contained £18,000, for a memorial stone — and what a lovely memorial stone I bought with it!' said Mary, polishing her new diamond ring on her cashmere sweater.

In life, the family may be a grim audience, whose faults should be mentioned only in private. But when referred to in public after their death, let their memorials be polished with praise.

So if you must address a family festivity, prepare for the best. But recognize that while others may forget your errors, your family will cherish them. Like good wine, they will change and be greatly savoured, as they mature with age.

Index

90-635

Janner, g.

90-635